WHO'S IN CHARGE HERE, ANYWAY?

WHO'S IN CHARGE HERE, ANYWAY?
Reflections from a Life in Business

Adam Zimmerman

Stoddart

TORONTO · BUFFALO

Published in 1997 by
Stoddart Publishing Co. Limited

Distributed in Canada by
General Distribution Services Inc.
30 Lesmill Road
Toronto, Canada M3B 2T6
Tel. (416) 445-3333
Fax (416) 445-5967
e-mail Customer.Service@ccmailgw.genpub.com

Distributed in the United States by
General Distribution Services Inc.
85 River Rock Drive, Suite 202
Buffalo, New York 14207
Toll-free tel. 1-800-805-1083
Toll-free fax 1-800-481-6207
e-mail gdsinc@genpub.com

Cataloguing in Publication Data
Who's in charge here, anyway?: reflections from a life in business
Zimmerman, Adam H., 1927–

ISBN 0-7737-2990-9
1. Zimmerman, Adam H., 1927– . 2. Executives - Canada - Biography.
3. Noranda (Firm). 4. Noranda Forest. I. Title.

HD9764.C32Z55 1997 658.4'092 96-931252-1

Cover design: Pekoe Jones/Multiphrenia
Cover photograph: Peter Paterson
Text design: Tannice Goddard
Computer layout: Mary Bowness

Printed and bound in Canada

My privileged business life from which come these reminiscences is primarily the result of those who coached, trusted, and helped me. Of course there were many, but the six who stand out were Duncan Gordon, John Bradfield, Alf Powis, Gaston Pouliot, Dave Davenport, and Tim Kenny, to all of whom this book is dedicated.

Contents

Preface

This book contains reminiscences of the main events in my business life — or at least those that seem to have some relevance beyond the mere moment and from which some lessons can be drawn. I must explain what I've not covered. Most particularly, I've made scant mention of my friends, other than those from my business life. I must say, however, that I have many friends in many places with varied interests, backgrounds, and points of view. By reason of their diversity alone, perhaps, they rarely intersected with the daily realities of my business life, but they influenced and sustained me greatly through a good number of challenging moments.

Mention of a few may offend the many. My neighbours in Go Home Bay have been a part of my experience, as have my Ballantyne cousins and their husbands; David Wishart, who followed me both at Clarkson Gordon and Royal Roads; Ron MacFeeters, the corporate iconoclast whose retirement was enriched by publicly asking tough questions of his business friends; Bill and Joan Grierson, who have been a part of every architectural experience I've had; John Lawson, who quietly and successfully ran Roy Thomson Hall for many years in his spare time; Hal Jackman, whose exemplary duty as lieutenant-governor has been remarkable; Tuzo Wilson, the late great geophysicist; Art MacCallum, who gave me my first summer job at the Marathon pulp mill; the doctors Harris, Dewar, Bigelow, and Trusler, who made such huge marks in orthopaedic and heart surgery; Dave Copp and the Harris brothers, Irving and Don, whose leadership in education and personal strength respectively I admired; and most importantly, Terry Sheard, who has been my wise counsellor and partner in so many ways.

Then there were my schoolmates, like Bob Stevens, Mike Scott, Skee McClelland, Larry Goad, Don Macfarlane, Doug Everett, and especially John DesBrisay, that wisest of men. Last, but certainly not least, are new friends John Turner, Ray Smith, Frank de Wit, Bill Ardell, Bob Spilman, Bob Findlay, Howard Hart, Joe Farrell, Paul Douglas, David Marshall, Huck Henry, Tom Kierans, and Jim McSwiney, whose acquaintance through business has grown to a larger dimension. These men and their wives always provided the utmost in hospitality and the kind of fun that usually comes only with the friends of our youth. I could go on and on about these valued friends and others, but the essence is my belief that we all represent an amalgam of the friendships that strengthen, enrich, and amuse us, and without which our lives would be barren indeed.

———◆———

THERE ARE MANY PEOPLE TO THANK for their help on this book, but primary on the list are my assistant, Marnie Armitage, who has typed this so often she may think it hers, and Len Marquis, a former Noranda associate, who also provided the basics of two chapters and then some. Along the way, many others have played parts: Pat Best, who gave good instruction; Jan Tyrrwhit and Kimberly Noble, both of whom reviewed a draft and offered counsel; Richard White, who did much of the earlier research, and Andrew Gorman, who first went through the files.

In the end, this has been both a humbling and a learning experience. I hope the book may have some general interest; certainly I can assure the reader it is unlikely anything more will come from this pen for some time.

ADAM ZIMMERMAN
Toronto

Introduction

When visitors enter the Centre Block of the Parliament Buildings in Ottawa, helpful guides draw their attention to the stone carvings that seem to spring from the surrounding walls. The two-storey foyer of the House of Commons is particularly ornate in this regard. A decorative frieze runs all the way around it just below ceiling height. To get a closer look, you have to climb a flight of stairs to the gallery. Then you can plainly make out, set in the corners, the figures known as the Four Pillars of Canada — a miner, a logger, a fisherman, and a farmer. Only an oil driller is missing, but five corners are too much to hope for, even in so rich and varied a place as the nation's capital.

Note, if you will, that a carving of a businessman is nowhere to be found.

I am a businessman, but I would not wish to have my features chiselled into this frieze should the offer be made. Nor am I deluded enough to suppose that my career was in any real sense exceptional. I helped to build a company, and I'm proud of that, but I'm not a pivotal or historical figure, and far less a font of universal wisdom. Thousands of people have headed major corporations, and thousands more will follow. My transitory claim to fame is that I was intimately involved in enterprises that were vital in maintaining two of Canada's four pillars, as well as the fifth Johnny-come-lately. I'm proud of that, because to deal responsibly with the nation's natural resources seems to me a worthwhile and important calling.

I had ample opportunity to experience both the peaks and valleys of these resource-based industries. If pressed, I think that most of us would agree with the dictum attributed to Sophie Tucker: "I've been rich, and I've been poor, and rich is better." Peaks provide a preferable view, but my record was not one of unblemished success. My final years at the corporate helm were depressed indeed, so it's difficult for me to claim any accomplishments. A usually benevolent deity turned things down in what ought to have been my glory days. My only consolation is my belief that even God Himself could not have realized profits from the prices we were getting for natural resource products in most of the period from 1982 to 1992.

One might wonder if there is anything to be gained from the observations of the likes of me. I think yes, because few retired executives amuse themselves by writing, and I am confident that I experienced a lot of interesting and exemplary events. My performance as a speaker is still sought, and I continue to oblige mostly because I want to advance the notions that business is an honourable pursuit, that good and honest people are involved in business endeavours, and that beneficial things often happen as a result of their efforts.

I think that whatever degree of success I have achieved on the soapbox circuit is due in part to my willingness to challenge conventional attitudes. I never set out to annoy an audience, but I have said things that I knew would shake people and make them think.

Many believe that the idea of writing a book visits only those who are afflicted with too much time on their hands, massive egos, or an absolute belief in their own view of the world. Since my retirement, I've had the time, but not the requisite hubris or certainty. Nevertheless, I do think, perhaps immodestly, that I do have something to say. I've led a full and rewarding life, and had a wonderful time along the way. I never hated the thought of going to work. I made both money and friends and always felt that, in my own small way, I was helping the world go round. But I'm aware that my kind of linear career path, spending by far the greatest part of my adult years in the service of Noranda Inc. and its subsidiaries and affiliates, is a thing of the past. I'm proud of the fact that I maintained the loyalty of my subordinates, and that a large majority of the investments I recommended stood the test of time. Generally speaking, these investments paid off — they didn't have to be written down, written off, or taken out and burned. Over the long haul, and left free to exercise my own judgment, I made a profit more often than not, which I conceived to be my primary objective and obligation. In the process, the company built a major forest enterprise, Noranda Forest Inc.

Throughout my career with Noranda, I had no other goal firmly in mind, no grand design or sequence of five-year plans. I simply did my job as best I could, and the rest seemed to fall into place. When the presidency of Noranda Inc. came my way in 1982, I accepted it gladly, because it seemed to represent the ultimate approval of my employers and my peers, but I never sought or consciously worked toward it. So this is by no means a how-to book; I have no secrets that, adopted bright and early tomorrow morning, will put anyone's star in instant ascendency. Zigzagging or corporation-hopping my way to fame and fortune according to the latest management theory was alien to me. Nor is what you're about to read a Noranda Inc. corporate history, a task I leave to other, more dispassionate hands. Nor is it really an autobiography, although much of it is written in the first person. When I left my office of thirty-odd years, my assistant, the invaluable Marnie Armitage, asked me what I wanted to do with the files. My first instinct was to throw them out. I was told, gently but firmly, that there were almost one hundred boxes full. I suspected that eighty percent of them should be shredded or consigned to the flames, but I had no idea which ones. Nor did I have the strength of mind to weed through them all. So I took the coward's way out. I had them moved to my country retreat and stacked in the lower level of a small outbuilding — to be exact, in the area where, as my next project, my grandson informs me I must install a pool table.

Now that I've examined the files, I can see that my first reaction was quite wrong. In fact, only five percent of their contents are in any way dear to me. Another bunch might plausibly find a home in the corporate archives, if such existed, but most are simply pieces of paper, and there's more than enough paper floating around the world. If anything, the files reveal an extraordinary consistency (some would say obstinacy) on my part as I struggled in every arena against what I viewed as governmental expediency and uninformed public-policy decisions.

I found myself reviewing more than three decades' worth of reports, appeals, meeting notes, recommendations, and policy statements of every stripe. From my standpoint, the responses from various levels of government were just as consistent as I was. There seemed throughout to be a shocking absence of rational process that would have enabled the best possible decisions to be reached by enlisting the aid of independent and informed advice. Rational process by definition develops sound data. Once such data are at hand, the good old-fashioned dialectic — thesis, antithesis, and synthesis — can get under way, and sound conclusions can be reached. Break the chain, and the result will be much less than it should have been — as the files proved, over and over again. Perhaps by sharing my experiences when it came to contacts with government, the media, the environmental movement, and other forces, I can demonstrate that Canadians easily could and should make fundamental changes in the way public policy is formulated and acted upon.

———✦———

AS I REFLECT ON THE DOMINANT FIGURES in my life — chief among them my father and John Bradfield, Noranda Inc.'s president when I came aboard — I'm reminded of E. P. Taylor.

4

Taylor was something of a legend in his time — founder of Argus Corp. (through which he and his pals controlled a lot of companies such as Domtar and Massey Ferguson) and creator of Canadian Breweries. In the 1950s, as a chartered-accounting student in the employ of Clarkson Gordon, I was assigned to work on the audit of Taylor's private affairs. These consisted mainly of the Windfields and National Stud farms, out of which the Toronto suburb of Don Mills evolved.

Taylor, like me latterly, had an office-in-outbuilding on his property. It held him, his private secretary, and his accountant. I sat at a table just outside his office door and could easily eavesdrop on his telephone conversations, which he was clearly happy to have me do. I remember one occasion when Taylor was personally negotiating a bank loan for, if memory serves, something in the realm of $5 million. Taylor wanted to get an interest rate of something like four and a quarter percent, even though he knew the bank would hold out for four and a half. The conversation began with the usual pleasantries and a full description of the purpose of the loan. Taylor stressed that since his asset base was huge, he was a credit-worthy borrower and expected to obtain a favourable interest rate. Of course he said little of his debt or cash flow, which I don't remember as being notably robust. The bank came back exactly as expected, but Taylor wasn't about to take it lying down. He put on a performance worthy of Olivier, hinting at the dire consequences that would surely befall if he didn't get the rate he wanted. Which of course he did and came away with a huge smile on his face. Actually, given the state of his finances at the time, I suspect that he'd have agreed to three and a half and more, but the force of his personality was something to be reckoned with, and the absolute assurance of his manner stuck with me always.

For me, this reflection illuminates how quickly and completely the business world changes. There may not be all that much new under the sun, but the players have changed beyond recognition.

Unless you are more or less my age (sixty-nine at the time of writing), or an avid student of corporate genealogy, you will quite probably have never heard of many of the people who were very important at the time I began my career. Some of the firms they established still bear their names, but beyond that, the men — they were almost exclusively men (and that's changing too) — have long since faded from memory. E. P. Taylor and K. C. Irving are perhaps exceptions to this rule, but few people today could identify with certainty the likes of John Prentice, Walter Koerner, Roy Jodrey, Bud MacDougald, Eric Phillips, Jim Duncan, Frank Sobey, Edgar Burton, Bill Arbuckle, or James Muir, and thirty others I could name if it mattered. Fame is fleeting, fortunes have their ups and downs, business goes on in constantly changing form and nothing is forever. The only constant *is* change, a fact familiar to every manager and certainly to me, because I weathered my share.

In any case, what relevance do the experiences of past titans and, more to the point, of Adam Hartley Zimmerman, have to the present day? My duties at Noranda were straightforward. I was part of the process where minerals were taken from the earth and trees cut down for the manufacture of useful products. Like it or not, these activities are integral to the nation's well-being. The forest sector is Canada's largest net exporter by far. Our resource industries are central to the economy of almost every community in the land. They directly employ something in the neighbourhood of one and a half million Canadians from sea to sea — double that number if you include all manner of secondary employment. Those who rise to the upper echelons of these industries are privileged to be in touch on an almost daily basis with events at the highest political and economic levels.

When it came to travel (and heaven knows it did), I logged countless hours in the air, which if nothing else impressed on me an intimidating sense of the country's scale. I often wondered how my predecessors managed to do what they did against almost insurmountable odds, back in the days when the nation was being developed from scratch. That it was indeed developed, that things indeed got done, reflects the fact that people and organizations, if left on their own, can define the tasks at hand and bring them to a successful conclusion.

Once I happened to be aboard the same long-drawn-out flight as Ray Smith, then president of MacMillan Bloedel. We were what you might call wary friends, because Noranda Forest had recently acquired a controlling interest in his firm and I'd been named chairman of it. I was in an introspective mood and remarked to Smith that I felt enlightened and enriched because my responsibilities took me constantly all across the land, from British Columbia to New Brunswick. This travel, I said, had not only brought me a wealth of experience, contributing greatly to my knowledge and understanding, but it enabled me to represent the firm's interests, wherever they were, from a much broader perspective than might otherwise have been possible. Surely, I added, he must feel much the same way.

Smith looked at me and laughed. "You," he said, "are the epitome of the 'effing' Eastern establishment."

I was stunned, not by Smith's language, but by his scornful dismissal of what I truly believed. I spent the next few minutes wondering whether I did in fact personify the much maligned and largely illusory establishment. More particularly, I wondered whether I was viewed by the staff of MacMillan Bloedel as a kindly caretaker (as I'd hoped) or as someone who'd been parachuted in. I concluded that Smith was expressing the extreme though understandable frustration of people who toil outside what are perceived to be the centres of power and influence and imagine they're being manipulated by forces from afar. But I thought then, and think now, that Smith was wrong. I can honestly state that never in my experience with Noranda did any consideration prevail except the good of whatever operation was concerned. We never robbed Peter to pay Paul.

Smith may have erred in his belief that I exemplified the apex of the Eastern establishment, but my personal history does have some relevance for the reader beginning this book. At January, 1997, I am sixty-nine, a senior executive turned senior citizen. I've lived through any number of economic ups and downs, gaining experience in organizing major operations on efficient, cost-competitive bases. I've played a role in the creation of many brand-new enterprises and taken old ones apart and put them together again. I've been embroiled in precedent-setting disputes and witnessed the adjustment of corporate values in response to the environmental movement. I've had my share of dealings with the media and tried to treat them as I wished to be treated. I've travelled widely and gained some appreciation of the way business is done on foreign shores. I've been on both sides of the takeover game, as predator and prey. I've sat on the boards of many companies and learned a little about the theory and practice of corporate governance. Like many others in the resource industries, I've had the mostly frustrating experience of sustained contact with governments, both federal and provincial.

I'm not much of a historian, but I do know that Canada's natural resources have long served as a metaphor for the nation. Diverse, scattered, and inaccessible, they are rich in potential but demand hard work and dedication to realize their promise; they are vulnerable unless treated with competence and care, at the mercy of forces beyond our borders, and at risk of misuse from within. I also know that no less an authority than Sir John A. Macdonald once declared, "We are recklessly destroying the timber of Canada, and there is scarcely a chance of replacing it." He was rushing his fences a bit, but I'll agree that, when he spoke, we ran the risk of taking both timber and Canada for granted. I wonder what Sir John A. would say, if he could be magically transported forward in time — perhaps that we took any number of chances along the way, but that somehow, against all odds, both the pillars of the country and the country itself still stand.

1

Funny Things Happened on the Way to Noranda

I'm not sure why I went to Trinity College at the University of Toronto, except that many of my friends were going there, so I figured I might as well go along for the ride. At the time I had no compelling ambition. I'd spent the previous eight years in the highly disciplined academic environments of Ridley College and Royal Roads (the Royal Canadian Naval College), and Trinity spelled, if nothing else, liberation and stimulation, a whole new range of possibilities. I enjoyed the parties, to which I drove in a 1927 funeral hearse because it was the only thing I could afford. The Second World War had barely ended, and there weren't many vehicles of any description on the lots. My uncle, who owned a printing business, had used the hearse as his wartime delivery van, so my buddy John DesBrisay (now a noted Toronto lawyer) and I seized the opportunity to ride in somewhat macabre style. Unfortunately the hearse was subject to fits and (less frequently) starts. One night we succeeded in snapping the driveshaft, and it went to the boneyard.

Walking did me good; it kept me in shape for the intramural athletic program, which included hockey, swimming, English rugger, and above all, football. None of my high school classmates would have bet a nickel that I'd stand on guard for the Varsity Blues, but I did.

I was undeniably a child of relative privilege. My family wasn't what you'd consider wealthy, but we certainly weren't poor. My ancestors exhibited an even, respectable record of accomplishment, unblemished by excess, although they managed to produce one or two black sheep.

My father, whose first name was also Adam although most people called him Hartley, was a mining engineer. His first job was at the Hollinger Mine in Timmins, Ontario, from 1924 to 1928. He brought his bride to the first brick house in town in 1925. I was born two years later, and my sister, Nancy, followed in 1931, by which time the family had lived briefly in Vancouver, where Dad was engaged in geological exploration. Then the depression landed in earnest, and he changed fields, joining what would later become Moore Corporation. Dad was associated with the company's U.S. operations, so we lived in Youngstown and Niagara Falls, New York, from 1930 until 1941, and I went through the American public school system. When it came time for junior high, my parents thought I'd better go back to Canada, where they believed they'd return someday. So I was sent to my maternal grandmother in Toronto, who lived just three blocks from Upper Canada College, which I attended for two years. After Canada entered the war, Dad headed for Ottawa, becoming first the director of Small Arms Production and then the director-general of Signals Production, which translates as radio and radar. I transferred to Ridley College in St. Catharines, Ontario, then, four years later — as the next best thing to enlisting, for which I was too young — to Royal Roads in

Victoria, British Columbia, for a final two years before the mast. I thought I'd have a fine time learning the skills of a naval officer while sailing around Vancouver Island — which I did, aboard various training vessels. The deal was that, if you survived the rigours of training and didn't fall overboard, you either went on to the permanent force or paid tuition and stayed with the Naval Reserve for five or six years. Eventually I became a lieutenant in the reserve.

At Trinity I took what was called "sock and fill" — Social and Philosophical studies. I'd never heard of most of the subject matter, but I was fortunate in that my "religious knowledge" (then a compulsory course) professor was Derwyn Owen, later the provost of Trinity, an extraordinarily articulate man whose profound grasp of history made the subject seem very simple. Owen brought alive for me all manner of different religions, and thus, all manner of different ways that different people looked at different issues. I'd never given these matters much thought, and if I later displayed tolerance for different ways of going about business and the greater business of life, I owed it in large part to Owen's teachings and example.

At the same time, I lucked into the classes taught by George Edison, who also became my tutor. His subjects were principally philosophy and ethics, with emphasis on Plato and Aristotle. Edison coined the immortal phrase "a comprehensive background of ignorance," a condition I suppose I exemplified at the time. But I appropriated the phrase, as did others he taught, and used it (rather intolerantly, come to think of it) at every opportunity. Edison practised the dialectic method better than anyone I've ever met. He encouraged us to adopt and defend opposing views, then move rationally to a synthetic conclusion. In a word, he taught us how to think in the fullest sense.

Another formative influence was Marcus Long, who taught logic at University College. Once he entered the classroom by squeezing himself in over the transom, rather than using the door like ordinary mortals. He did so to impress on us the idea that what you expect to happen sometimes doesn't. His bravura classroom antics, if nothing else, helped open a window in my mind.

In spite of today's penchant for rewarding MBAs with the top jobs, I still endorse the idea of a good, old-fashioned liberal-arts education as the basis for a successful career in almost any business. It certainly adds perspective to your outlook. You learn that the individual is a very small cog in a very big wheel, and that there's more to life than a balance sheet. I could name a lot of people who play leading roles in industry but whose narrowness boggles the mind. They see business only as numbers and measure success in pounds of concrete or feet of steel or units of production. Human frailty does not enter their equations. I don't pretend to be an intellectual, but thanks to my professors, I emerged from Trinity convinced that the people who've truly changed the world seldom have their noses firmly affixed to the corporate grindstone.

And so, replete with these broadening though not necessarily rewarding speculations, I graduated in 1950 as a philosophy major with a general-arts degree. Because I was considered a navy veteran, thanks to Royal Roads, I could take a four-year degree in three, so my fourth year was more or less postgrad. I hung around, attending a mix of classes and getting to know my future wife. The trouble was that an arts degree, along with a ticket, got you aboard a bus. I still didn't know what I wanted to do in the working world. Certainly the job market was thin. My father advised me as best he could, but we'd led rather separate lives. Although he was reasonably well connected, he hadn't imparted all that much in the way of business lore. He did say, "It doesn't matter what you do. Just do it as hard and as well as you can, and the future will unfold as it should." And he was absolutely right, or so it proved in my case.

More than anything, Dad convinced me of the wisdom of working hard, fully studying an issue, and taking time so that the correct decision could emerge. He would rarely force a resolution to a problem and to my knowledge didn't make many bad calls. By the time he retired in 1967 he'd become chairman of Canada's Defence Research Board, having overseen the launching of Canada's first communications satellite and the navy's first hydrofoil.

I crossed off my options one by one. Teaching never even entered my mind. Medicine, engineering, and law held minimal appeal. Business of some undefined stripe seemed the way to go, and I went so far as to apply to Harvard Business School. A friend and I took the train to Boston and were interviewed by a man who asked what I thought was going to happen to the world. I volunteered the view that many countries would turn toward socialism. We had a long chat about the redistribution of wealth, and I didn't get accepted. I've always admired that fellow for rejecting me. He was absolutely correct: I'd have been a bad candidate at that time. I would have struggled every inch of the way, I wouldn't have taken to what they had to offer, and I'd probably have rushed madly off and redistributed wealth for the rest of my days.

Instead, like other U. of T. grads, I threw myself on the mercies of the corporate recruiters who swarmed the campus every spring. Procter and Gamble paid the highest salaries and were said to teach a junior trainee the most in the least possible time. And so, faced with the need to earn a living and bearing in mind the Hobbesian view that the life of man in the state of nature is solitary, poor, nasty, brutish, and short, I pledged myself to the task of selling soap to 532 grocery stores in and around Chatham, Ontario.

Surprisingly, I could sell soap, but I realized in the first hour that it wasn't going to sustain me intellectually. Fortunately I was rescued five months later in October 1950. Someone had described me to Duncan Gordon of Clarkson, Gordon and Co., chartered accountants, at a cocktail party as a young man with a decent education, but with scant hope of getting a decent job because I couldn't do anything useful. As it turned out, Duncan and his brother, Walter, were mulling over the novel idea of hiring a couple of trainees who held something other than a commerce degree. In the event, they chose me and Michael MacKenzie, a classmate at Trinity, as guinea pigs. Mike stayed with Clarkson Gordon, became a partner, and was later named superintendent of Financial Institutions for Canada, so there must have been something to the experiment, which at the time seemed a long shot. It certainly didn't cost much; my starting salary was roughly half what I'd received for peddling Ivory, Duz, Oxydol, Tide, and Kirk's Hardwater Castille.

In fact, the big winners were Michael and me, because we were pulled through the Clarkson Gordon finishing school for young, upwardly mobile WASPs. The Gordon brothers and their partners represented (by their client base) and embodied (in themselves) the aristocracy of the Canadian business world.

Walter Gordon, the elder brother, was a man of the greatest integrity and ability. He'd attempted to enlist during the Second World War, but was rejected as physically unfit; instead, he served as a bureaucrat in the Wartime Prices and Trade Board before assuming the leadership of the family firm, which had been founded in the 1920s by his father H. D. L. Gordon and Geoffrey Clarkson. Walter had no particular interest in accounting per se. He did, however, make extremely shrewd personnel decisions, taking into the Clarkson Gordon partnership such men as Grant Glassco, Alec Adamson, Jack Wilson, and George Richardson. Confident they would mind the store, he branched off into management consulting, forming another company with one of his friends — J. D. Woods and Gordon. Initially concerned with time-and-motion studies, it evolved into what's now the consulting arm of Ernst and Young. Realizing that many older family firms were on rocky ground because of high taxes and succession duties, Walter then formed Canadian Corporate Management, an investment holding company, in partnership with Grant Glassco. CCM liquidated financially troubled family-owned businesses and merged them within their public company. They had a good run, but eventually wound up with a dog's breakfast of disparate firms, with the result that CCM disintegrated.

A stalwart Liberal, Walter went on to a bittersweet political career as minister of finance in the Pearson government and president of the Privy Council.

Duncan Gordon shared his older brother's integrity and self-confidence, but seemed by comparison introspective and shy. I worked directly for him, and he became a good friend, adviser, and mentor, or perhaps exemplar. He blossomed as his responsibilities and authority grew after Walter moved into politics. He remained a bachelor and had many cultural as well as business interests. But he saw to it that the firm kept on going and growing, and was on top of every detail. He carried a notepad filled with cryptic memoranda and never forgot a thing. Almost ruthless when the need arose, he made blunt appraisals of a client's shortcomings and weeded out his own shop as well. He hired me — but he also told me, when the time came, that I'd probably do better outside the accounting field.

Duncan Gordon was a true humanitarian and became a mainstay of the Hospital for Sick Children. In concert with John Law, its president at the time, he set new standards of successful fund-raising, enabling the hospital to pursue its groundbreaking research programs. After Law's premature death, Duncan more or less took charge. He brought me to the hospital's board of trustees (where I remained for twenty-two years) and saw to it that I was appointed treasurer.

But I'm getting decades ahead of myself. In 1950 each raw recruit at Clarkson Gordon was issued a name tag, a green pencil, and a rubber thimble, the kind bank tellers use to count money. Our job was to conduct external audits of plant offices. At the time my level of financial sophistication stopped short at balancing my cheque-book. The wonders of double-entry bookkeeping came as a rude surprise. We examined invoices for propriety and cheques for completeness, saw that ledgers were all correct and accounted for, matched them and added up the columns. This, with only minor variations, occupied us for two solid years. In the evenings we did our lessons — a rigorous correspondence course conducted through

Queen's University. It was hard slogging to earn the right to put C.A. after our names — a three- or four-year articling procedure as a student in accounts, punctuated by exams — and we had to do a lot of things that might seem repetitious and unnecessary today. Our training was methodical and rigid. The rules were understood, the ethic absolute. We learned the virtues of endless patience and attention to detail. On a practical level, we had the priceless opportunity to become familiar with the inside operations of diverse businesses and to meet the people who ran them.

Some of these people became good friends. I think particularly of Jack Rhind, whom I would later succeed as chairman of Confederation Life; Richard Rohmer, the now famous author, lawyer, and military man; Charlie Dubin, Ontario's retired chief justice; Bill Broadhurst, who ran Price Waterhouse; and Don Mingay, who eventually retired from selling insurance and founded Creemore Springs Brewery.

It was a small world and led inevitably to what could be described as an old boys' network. Did I keep bumping into my Upper Canada and Ridley and Trinity classmates on my way up the ladder? The answer is: yes, I met them socially, but no, virtually never in business. Naturally I accumulated a lot of former schoolmates and people who remembered me, with varying degrees of affection, from various playing fields. In the 1950s there was a finite number of places for young would-be movers and shakers to congregate. We weren't yet ready for the York Club; there were a few restaurants that catered to the promising but relatively penniless — the Stoodleigh, the Shakespeare, the King Edward Hotel cafeteria, and a place called Child's, where you could eat for a dollar. We staked out a regular table and plotted to someday rule the world, between wondering where the next dollar was coming from.

As the years passed, I was never hired or promoted by — or even worked with — anyone who was part of a hereditary network. I kept plenty of friends, but that's because our careers had intermeshed, more or less by accident. Despite Ray Smith's assertion, the notion of the Establishment is vague and unprovable. My friends are simply a mix of surprisingly disparate people who happened to meet at a particular point in time. We moved on to better things, but we didn't succeed in forming some sort of cabal that fixed the course of events to suit our predetermined design. In the business I would eventually become involved in, this so-called network meant nothing. (Perhaps it was different in the legal or financial fields. The bright young lawyers saw more of one another as they marched toward the bench. And I imagine that, if someone's father owned a brokerage, the fact may have led to a better job than might have surfaced on the open market.)

In these early years I focused on trying to satisfy my new employers and keep my head amid a blaze of unfamiliar tasks, with varying results. I joined Clarkson Gordon in the fall of 1950, married Janet in the spring of 1951, and promptly failed my first-year accounting exams the following September. This event reflected both the pleasant distractions of marriage and the disquieting fact that I knew bugger-all about business.

When I look back, notwithstanding my lasting regard for the Gordons, the titans of industry tend to recede from view, and tangential personalities bubble to the surface. For some reason I remember the pastimes of a fellow C.A. student named Kazi Ahmed — the exception who proved the WASP rule. One day he and I, along with several other staffers, were assigned the mind-numbing task of counting securities in the bowels of the Bank of Commerce, where we sat, sifting through a good chunk of the nation's wealth as represented by share certificates.

If you want a glimpse of ridiculously florid art, I suggest a look at vintage 1950s shares. Most of the certificates featured gleaming and impressive factories arising from the sea, descending from the clouds, or (prophetically) popping up amid forest glades. Some featured the spirit of enterprise making imperial gestures. Usually this spirit was portrayed as an amply endowed young woman draped in patriotic bunting, but with her bosom almost totally exposed. Naturally a contest developed among the young and restless auditors as to who could boast the most scantily clad female figures. Kazi, however, decided to take matters one step further, by red-pencilling their nipples, on the theory that no one but cage clerks was ever likely to spy his handiwork. But he was wrong. A bank official took both notice and umbrage, and the hapless Kazi was reassigned to the task of reviewing an insurance brokerage's accounts receivable.

This new duty, which involved checking the posting of invoices and payments in a ledger, required that he be given a work space. This proved to be the office of the president, off sunning himself in some more salubrious clime. Alas, Kazi became unnaturally fascinated by the president's potted rubber plant. Its thick and glossy leaves proved too much of a temptation, and Kazi for reasons known only to himself carved his initials into one of the fronds. Regrettably the president was not a former member of Kappa Alpha, and Kazi's guilt was, you might say, writ large. No doubt he went on to a glowing career in an artists' colony, or perhaps an advertising agency — but his predilection for defacing clients' property was one of several factors that hastened his departure from the Clarkson Gordon ranks.

A rather more serious breach of conduct in which I soon found myself embroiled was the so-called "highways scandal" of 1953. Ontario, along with other provinces, was hastening to complete the Trans-Canada Highway. This involved both building brand-new stretches and upgrading existing routes. But road-building is an inexact science, offering wide scope for chicanery and graft. Estimates (read: shots in the dark) were the order of the day, and only a final survey could determine value for money spent. This exercise was impeded by the fact that the surveys had been fudged past all belief. The fraud was based on what was known as classification — simply put, what percentage of the materials moved around a given worksite was solid rock and what percentage was earth or gravel. Contracts were awarded on the basis of different rates for each. For instance, a roadbed might be assumed to be composed of sixty percent earth at two dollars a yard and forty percent rock at more than twice that figure. Nobody knew for sure what was actually the case except the on-site engineers. As a result, inventive minds turned to the production of false surveys that altered the proportions of different materials, thus vastly inflating the monies billed to the government.

To thwart these schemes, Clarkson Gordon staffers paired up with Department of Highways Ontario engineers and began to tour the province. I went with a man named Alex Mantle all over the northerly regions, from Kenora to Owen Sound. We would arrive without warning at a contract site, seal all the drawings and survey books, and subject them to an instant audit. We soon found gross discrepancies — one survey went into great detail concerning gravel where none in fact existed. Elsewhere we actually seized documents labelled HQ (honest quantities) and BQ (bastard quantities), a none-too-subtle clue that something was amiss. As you might expect, we soon wore out our welcome. Sometimes we were refused access until a search warrant was presented on our behalf by a police officer. At one site the resident engineer chased me round and round a car for fifteen minutes, throwing ineffectual punches into the air.

A third eye-opener took place in Port Arthur (now Thunder Bay), the epicentre of the investigation. We met there one evening with several lawyers and senior representatives of both Clarkson Gordon and the DHO. I walked into a hotel room where these men had already poured themselves a round of drinks and immediately saw a holstered revolver lying on the bed. This proved to be the property of none other than David Humphrey, a budding criminal lawyer who later became a noted judge. Humphrey thought himself a possible target of the underworld and wanted at least to go down fighting! Also present, though not, as I recall, armed to the teeth, was Charles Dubin, today a retired chief justice of Ontario. The friendship begun at that moment has endured.

An infinity of audits isn't the most spine-tingling or anecdotally rich of human endeavours, so I'll spare you further details, other than to say I rose in the Clarkson Gordon ranks to audit supervisor, the equivalent of today's audit manager. Notwithstanding this recognition, my personality and interests were drawing me elsewhere.

Providentially, in 1958 the opportunity arose to kill two birds with one stone. The first bird was an outstanding bill that had been sent by Woods Gordon, the firm's consulting arm, to John Bradfield, the president of Noranda Mines Limited. Bradfield had commissioned a study to aid him in dragging the company's financial management practices into the latter half of the twentieth century. One recommendation called for the creation of a comptroller's function, where before there'd been none. Bradfield thought this sounded fairly reasonable and said, "I'll pay you what we owe, but not until you find me the guy."

And so the second bird was me.

I had no idea what I was getting into. At the time I'd had some degree of contact with a number of other mining accounts, but never with Noranda Mines. The whole thing, on the face of it, sounds rather implausible: becoming a forestry mogul by first joining an accounting firm and then moving to a mining company? In any event I was sent packing to the firm that would employ me, in one way or another, for the next thirty-five years.

2

From This Little Acorn . . .

As president of Noranda Mines in the late 1950s, John Bradfield had his work cut out for him, but he was equal to the task, a clear-thinking man who knew his company well.

The Noranda story begins in 1920, when Edmund Horne, a prospector in search of gold, staked out seventy acres of bush and muskeg in Rouyn Township, in northwestern Quebec. Gold was there, but as a byproduct of a large and fantastically rich deposit of copper that was quickly exploited by a syndicate of twelve men to whom Horne and his associates sold their interests. This syndicate evolved into an incorporated company, one member of which had a secretary with a flair for abbreviation, which is how "Northern Canada" became "Noranda."

Bradfield arrived, along with fellow engineer Richard Porritt, in

1926, with the plans for the first copper smelter tucked beneath his arm. He hiked down a corduroy road into the bush and slept in a log shanty. He later built the smelter, got it into production and served as plant engineer until 1938, when he contracted pneumonia. His recuperation involved a transfer to Toronto, where he was appointed corporate secretary, from which perch he very quickly learned to run the entire enterprise, top to bottom.

In 1928 Noranda turned its first operating profit — a modest $3-million. It would continue to see the numbers come up black for the next fifty-four years. By 1939, under the presidency of J. Y. Murdoch, one of the company's original founders, Noranda Mines was Canada's second-largest copper producer and third-largest gold-mining concern. But most of the corporate eggs were lodged in a single basket — the original Horne Mine, the lifespan of which was even then finite. Ore bodies are a wasting asset; they start to die from the day the first tonne of rock is hoisted to the surface. Noranda had been reasonably successful when it came to processing raw materials into finished products, but the need for further diversification was plain to all.

By the early 1950s the accepted wisdom was that Noranda Mines was moribund, making money in spite of unimaginative corporate leadership and a president who by then was waging a battle with alcohol. Murdoch's ever more frequent lapses left a gaping hole, which Bradfield fortunately filled. Indeed, in 1956, the directors bowed to the inevitable and named him the company's second president. At this time he presided over the Horne and Waite Amulet mines in Quebec, three gold mines in the Timmins area, the Gaspé Copper Mine, Canada Wire and Cable, Canadian Copper Refiners, and Noranda Copper and Brass. The firm was running an $18-million profit after taxes, but nobody knew where the money was coming from or how long it could last.

Bradfield wanted to modernize the company and staff it for the future. He hired me, Alf Powis, Peter Riggin, Ozzie Hinds, Keith

Hendrick, and Ken Cork, and did this basically on his own initiative; he didn't need headhunters or batteries of psychological tests. He picked us well, and he expected us to do what he himself had done. If we saw a ball, we were to pick it up and head for the nearest goal line. He was a man of unfailing loyalty to his people, consideration for others in general, and tremendous drive for his company to succeed. He never stood on ceremony. Not a believer in endless reports and studies, he would sit down and listen patiently to everyone's point of view, then decide who'd put forward the best proposition. In some cases, the decision came as a result of a collegial discussion process. We were given free rein; he enjoyed watching us go. He was, for me, the perfect boss — a straight-shooting engineer cum corporate titan whose shrewd choice of personnel and farsighted game plan transformed a potentially waning mining company into an industrial giant. He remained at the helm for twenty-five years, finally relinquishing his title in 1968.

But at the time he hired me Noranda Mines was in the Dark Ages when it came to financial reporting. Its internal procedures were inadequate for the company it had become. The Woods Gordon study had identified the need for a comptroller's function, and rightly so; previously there'd been only a treasurer who, along with two other staffers, handled the accounting.

What I knew about mining at that time was fairly rudimentary, and so it made sense to name me assistant comptroller; they didn't want to give a neophyte outsider full responsibility. My boss, Cliff Muir, was a blinkered workaholic who also served as director of sales (his real job). I had a bit of an edge because he hadn't much idea what a comptroller should do; nonetheless he questioned my every move.

There were three main challenges at hand. First, Noranda Mines had no system for capital appropriations and allocations. Everything was done on a back-of-the-envelope basis. People who wanted to buy or build something would corner Dick Porritt (by then the firm's vice-president and general manager) or Bill Roscoe (also a vice-president and former engineer) at a cocktail party and say they needed 300,000 bucks for this or that. Maybe they'd get it; maybe they wouldn't. If they did, there was plenty more where it came from — the company was loaded. The trick was to keep track of it, which nobody had then been mandated to do.

My second project was to set up some sort of budgeting process so that we'd have an informed idea of what we were expected to do the next year. The third was to regularize the operational reporting so that everyone submitted financial results in a uniform and cogent way. All this had previously gone on, although in a rather haphazard fashion; there'd certainly been an accounting function of some description. But things were so scattered that Bradfield admitted that even he was often in the dark.

The task was actually pretty straightforward once we got down to it, although we divided the responsibility in an unconventional way. The treasurer and I were separate but equal. He did money and banking, while I handled taxation, accounting, budgeting, and — occasionally — litigation. We also had to identify the right people and get them slotted.

Now that someone was actually charged with getting a handle on the accounts, one of the first things I had to deal with was the legal aftermath of the Gaspé Copper strike. Briefly put, Gaspé Copper Mines had begun production in 1955 off in the wilds of Murdochville, Quebec (the company town, named for J. Y. himself). This was a most forbidding stretch of countryside, marked by the unattractively named Shickshock Mountains. Premier Maurice Duplessis, who headed the Union Nationale government, had brought in hydroelectric power by running a cable under the Gulf of St. Lawrence into Baie Comeau, then stringing transmission wires two hundred kilometres overland. The St. Lawrence crossing was managed by Noranda's subsidiary, Canada Wire and Cable, and regrettably it was unsuccessful in the long term. There was a road link to Gaspé town, the nearest railhead, one hundred kilometres away. The snowfall was unbelievable; vehicles were buried beneath huge drifts and crushed by passing ploughs. The town was laid out in the typical company-town fashion of the day, stretching up a steep hillside that became a quagmire when it thawed. I found it grim and depressing, and I suppose the workers did, too.

The mine workers were young and poorly educated unskilled labourers who'd previously been seasonal fishermen and lumberjacks. Their idea of a steady job was something that occupied them for a month or so, after which they could go hunting. They were also badly led. After a few false starts they wound up represented by the United Steelworkers of America, which at the time was a hellfire union with a taste for confrontation. Rhetoric escalated into violence, and the strike began in March 1957. While the grounds for the strike seemed flimsy, the strike itself was the obvious manifestation of grievances that were real but not understood at the time.

Management went to the mattresses inside the plant. It was more like a siege than a strike. The company tried to air-drop supplies to the people holed up there. The pilots came in low, buzzing the beleaguered compound, and aiming for the smelter stack as if they were on a bombing run. They certainly caught flak — the strikers shot at them with deer rifles. Workers who refused to join the strike were beaten, their homes vandalized, and their families terrorized.

The strike went on for seven months and became a province-wide cause célèbre. René Lévesque, in his capacity as a CBC Television journalist, came to town with an antimanagement chip on his shoulder, but didn't like the rough stuff and fled. One suspects that Lévesque confirmed an anti-Anglo, anticorporate bias that stayed with him thereafter. When he was premier, he stood Bradfield up for a meeting in Quebec City that had long been arranged.

Pierre Trudeau, too, then the editor of Cité Libre, took up the strikers' cause in the magazine. Violence spread to the Port of Montreal, where the captain of a ship carrying copper to Noranda's refinery was injured by a mob. A fuel-storage depot was blown up with stolen dynamite, and a striker who tried to sabotage the plant itself blew himself to bits. The town was placed under curfew, Duplessis sent reinforcements to aid the local Quebec Provincial Police, and the strike ended, bitterly, in August, amid charges of rampant union-busting and collusion between Noranda and the provincial government. I'm glad to say that I missed out on all these events, having been quietly auditing the books of family businesses in rural Ontario towns from the Clarkson Gordon offices.

The Gaspé trial began in September 1960 in Quebec Superior Court. Despite being advised by the newly elected premier, Jean Lesage, to negotiate a settlement, Noranda had decided to press its suit against the United Steelworkers Union for $2.25-million in damages. In my role as comptroller, I was asked to figure out how much the company had lost as a result of the strike. There were two components involved in our claim: the actual damages to plant and property, which were fairly straightforward, and the loss represented by the value of the ore that we'd been unable to mine while the strike ran its course.

This exercise was more complex than one might think. The union's position was that, when it came to the ore, we hadn't lost much of anything. That is, it simply went unmined, and we could get to it on the day that full production resumed. Our position was that we'd lost what we would have realized for it, had we not been struck. We managed to prove that a tonne not mined today is unrealized until the end of the life of the mine, so its value compounds from the date unmined. The price of copper during the strike had gone up and down, but was on average much higher than shortly after it ended, and this tended to complicate our argument. There were other, rather more elegant calculations involved, as well, and it was my job to argue this case as best I could. I began my work on the case in January and got back home twice between then and April. It was a terrible winter, and I developed no great passion for Quebec City, even though I was camped out in comfort at the Château Frontenac.

I think I spent about ten hours, the second or third longest time of anyone in the witness box, although this was only a fraction of the effort by Bill Brissenden, the mine manager. There were more than 350 witnesses in all, who accounted for 200,000 pages of transcripts.

I was sweating buckets in the box, but I tried not to let it show, even though my wool suit was steaming. I learned several things from the experience. First, if you speak with real conviction, chances are you'll sound more or less convincing. Second, if you're well prepared — and we all studied day and night to prepare for our turn in the box — you're going to know many times more about the subject than the people who are grilling you. Even if you don't know the answer to a particular question, you're still a whole lot closer to it than they are, so there's nothing to be afraid of. It's not a matter of bullshitting, it's just a matter of facts, which you must have at your disposal. Never be diffident, as long as you know in your bones you've done your homework.

In the end the final settlement was in Noranda's favour, although not in the amount we'd claimed. The trial ended in October 1962, and we were awarded almost $1.75-million plus interest and costs for damages and lost profits. The judgment was appealed, and in 1967 it was upheld on appeal. Ultimately the case wound up in the Supreme Court, which in 1970 also found for the company. After more than a decade, the final cheque was about $2.5-million total. A nice sum to have in hand — but it went temporarily missing in transit. The union handed the cheque over to Brissenden in Montreal, who was so excited he spent several days wandering around town showing it to people who'd been involved in the trial. He then brought it to Toronto and had his picture taken before he realized it should have been deposited. We were losing a tidy sum in interest.

My involvement in the Gaspé trial taught me several lessons, among them how crucial personalities are in shaping events. Harty Bérubé, the mine's assistant manager, and Brissenden were strong-minded individuals with an absolute concept of right and wrong. I suppose if I'd been living in Murdochville at the time, I'd have been inclined to get pretty stiff-necked about the whole thing, too. Dick Porritt, Noranda's president at the time, was also an exponent of the hard line, possibly because when he'd been manager of the Horne Mine, he'd been roughed up by picketers. In any event the strike marked a low ebb in Noranda's labour-management relations, and both sides displayed a real lack of compromise, flexibility, and pragmatism.

No one was entirely guiltless in the Gaspé episode. The union leaders were self-serving toughs, while Noranda's executives clung to some antediluvian ideas. They'd been opposed to the union, and particularly the dues checkoff, from the outset. The company thought it knew best, but it didn't know enough to screen employees or treat them with the respect they deserved. They were guilty of paternalism at its worst. Duplessis was heavy-handed, no doubt, but he had no choice. He could have ceded the town to mob rule or done his duty and enforced the law. He chose the latter course, but too late — so the idea of Noranda and the provincial government in some unholy alliance gained currency and took a long time to die down.

In spite of all this, Noranda was able to engage two great lawyers who not only won the case but also became bonded in many ways thereafter to some of us who were involved. Gaston Pouliot, then a young and totally brilliant lawyer and strategist, became one of my greatest friends — eventually I suggested him as a Southam director, which he became, serving with distinction for some time. The other was Jean Martineau, a bâtonnier of the Quebec Bar and perhaps its leading lawyer. Intelligent, urbane, meticulous, and totally human, he led us all as counsel both in the courtroom and the Quebec City restaurants. These two men remain major figures in my experience.

The strike marked a watershed in the company's affairs. Its confrontational approach to unions moderated after that. Peter Riggin, a former lawyer who joined the firm as director of corporate affairs in 1957 with responsibility for labour and personnel, was a skilled negotiator, and he had a lot to do with turning things around.

Once the lawsuit had been settled, it was back to the office for me. Some people probably hadn't missed me, but there was work to be done. Don Schmitt in particular (then assistant manager at the Horne) had bucked my ideas when I first arrived on the scene. He didn't like having systematically to justify his capital expenditures or to detail his operating plans for the coming year. His instinctive reaction was, basically, here's this kid from Toronto trying to tell me how to run my business. In the end I think I was able to disarm him and others to a degree — but only to a degree, because I was in fact hired to tell people with many more years in the mining business than I had what to do with respect to accounting and reporting. These guys had been raised on the notion that the mine manager was king. They didn't want to be second-guessed, but some of them weren't good all-round managers, and the systems that we so clearly had to set in place would make their shortcomings evident. My peers and I represented a new dimension in management accountability. Together with Peter Riggin, Ken Cork, Alf Powis, and Gordon Driver, I was in at the beginning of the new Noranda of the 1960s and 1970s — at the transformation of a loose-knit string of one-mine outposts (complete with single-site mentality) into a modern corporate organization.

In the main, though, everyone went along, with the notable exception of Canadian Copper Refiners, the refinery subsidiary of Noranda. The manager, John Schoen, was a citadel unto himself and his assistant, John Pearce. His operations were opaque to everyone for many years. CCR was a prime example of why the new systems and controls were desperately needed. I never liked the place, because I couldn't come to grips with it. No one could, but my mandate was to grasp what was going on across the board, so that everyone's financial reporting was clear and clearly understood.

While I may have been feeling my way to some extent, I knew what had to be done and that the brass wanted it. I got to travel a lot, which was a great novelty, although hard on my family life. At

Clarkson Gordon I might have been gone for a week in Fergus or Barrie, Ontario, but now I was going much farther afield, meeting new people and seeing new things. I wanted to see even more. Which is why, in 1961, after my preparations for the lawsuit, my ears perked up when I heard that Alf Powis, then Bradfield's assistant, was heading west to check out a bankrupt forest company called National Forest Products. I was eager to visit British Columbia, the home of my youth, so I suggested to Powis that I'd like to join him when the dealing got serious, which it did in April 1961.

━━◆━━

AT THAT TIME PRINCE GEORGE, B.C., soon to be the centre of our new forest investment, had wooden sidewalks. I have a picture taken the day we landed there of Dave Davenport, our lawyer, and Powis in front of the terminal building. I remember thinking that I'd never before been so far away and so close to the edge of the frontier, and I wondered if I'd ever be back. Little did I know.

British Columbia was run by W. A.C. (Wacky, as he was often known) Bennett, the apostle of Social Credit, together with a cabinet of oddball characters. I had a particular interest in all B.C. premiers, as my great-uncle, T. Dufferin Pattullo, had held the office around 1940. The province's biggest economic asset was a thriving lumber industry, primarily on the coast, but pulp mills were few and far between. Inland they didn't exist. The entire Interior was covered with a permanent lingering haze — the smoke from countless "tepee burners," which burned wood waste and sawdust; there was no other way to get rid of the stuff. With the technology of the day, only half of the wood in a tree made lumber; the rest went up in smoke. The waste was profligate, an absolute crying shame. The Interior sawmills were primitive, located miles from anywhere on awful roads. They cut in low volume with equally low accuracy. Some of them were so small they could almost have been put on the back of a truck.

Many should have been; the owners made no money from them and couldn't wait to sell. What they had was "quota," a forest area gift from the province.

Noranda, undaunted, wanted to get its foot in the door. The Home Mine's days were numbered and we knew the virtues of diversity. We didn't know much about trees, except that they, like ore, were a natural resource and subject to provincial jurisdiction. We were prepared to learn, but it would be an expensive lesson, and a fairly complicated financial transaction loomed, which is why I flew out with Powis.

National Forest Products, then in receivership, had half a dozen sawmills, split between the Okanagan Valley (the Summerland Box Company, Tulameen Forest Products, and the Osoyoos and Oliver mills) and the Upper Fraser and Sinclair Spruce mills near Prince George. The latter were larger and slightly more successful. The former were worse than dogs, the most dreadful collection of old machinery chewing up good wood. We really bought a bag of bones, but we also bought something beyond price — the harvesting quota for the sawmills and a three-million-acre pulp-harvesting area that had been created by the provincial forestry minister, Ray Williston. This was an area preapproved for a pulp mill, which nobody showed any signs of wanting to build.

Williston's aim was to create a new order from long-standing chaos. Before his tenure, his department had been involved in some corruption and bribe-taking. Basically timber licences were being allotted to the party faithful for favours received. He moved quickly to establish a system that was more transparent and aboveboard. A forest company had to engage in public hearings and justify its occupation of a given site. Licences were granted after full debate and under far stricter conditions than previously. Williston also wanted to encourage firms to consolidate and enlarge their sawmills, which would then make practical the construction of facilities to chip and process the waste wood that had previously been burned. Nobody knew the volume of the chips that would then be produced, hence the pulp-harvesting areas, which would provide enough wood to feed a pulp facility if the waste-wood chip supply proved inadequate. Williston believed that a company with a timber-cutting licence might never have to actually harvest a single tree to feed its pulp mill. Instead, it could take the leftover wood that wasn't suitable for lumber — at the time anything measuring less than twelve inches in diameter at chest height — and ship it off to be pulped. In other words, the pulp industry could turn a profit by engaging in waste disposal on a giant scale. Some people thought he was crazy, but he was right, and we at Noranda were his allies.

At times I thought Williston was crazy, no question about it, but he was crazy like a fox. He was and is a real straight shooter, and he was determined to guard against the cronyism and graft that had plagued the forestry department before he came on the scene. He did this by cutting everyone else out of the loop. We'd sit in his office and he'd personally type the substance of the discussion on a tear-off memo pad. It never went to phalanxes of bureaucrats for long-drawn-out approval. He ran the forestry ministry like a fiefdom and certainly could have gotten away with murder, but he never seemed to favour one company over another. He made some bad calls, but the huge Interior B.C. pulp industry of today stands as testament to his ability and even-handedness.

National Forest Products had liabilities of a substantial order — a polite way of saying it was broke. The mills had been put together by an entrepreneur who owed money to all points of the compass. The CIBC held $3-million in loans; Traders Finance had claims on most of the logging equipment. Noranda offered the partners a payoff that would get rid of their debts, leaving them with a fifteen-percent interest in a million-dollar company.

All the other forest companies were waiting for the cherry to drop. They figured that National Forest would go directly into bankruptcy without passing Go, and that they could then pick up the pieces. But Noranda beat them to the punch, thanks in part to the efforts of the aforementioned Dave Davenport, a junior member of Noranda's Vancouver legal firm who'd been assigned to us because the senior partner was in Hawaii. Late one night, as the short strokes of the deal were in progress, we cooked up the notion that, in the event that there were undisclosed liabilities, we'd be paid for them, dollar for dollar, out of NFP's residual interest in the newly created company. We eventually unearthed something like $78,000 in liabilities they hadn't remembered to tell us about, so we offered cash for the remaining $72,000 of their $150,000 stake and wound up with one hundred percent control. National Forest Products was resurrected as Northwood Mills and open for business. It was April 1961.

I'd certainly credit Alf Powis with the foresight that got Noranda into the forest industry. Powis had joined the company shortly before I arrived, ostensibly as assistant treasurer. He'd been a financial analyst at Sun Life and soon began to function as Bradfield's aide-de-camp. Like many other business wizards I've encountered, he always carried a notebook filled with memoranda only he could decipher. Bradfield may have sown the seed for Noranda's diversification, but it was Powis who really planted it. We all subscribed to the notion and joined our efforts to this purpose. At first my input was quite routine and limited to the financial side, but pretty soon I knew a whole lot more than anybody else in Noranda about the forest industry. The industry came to feel like something I was destined to do. I understood it, I liked it, and I kept on liking it.

I was essentially free to move in this direction, because neither Alf Powis nor Ken Cork displayed much interest in operations per se. Maybe that's what set me apart — I liked the plants and the mills and the people who ran them. Later on, when we had holdings continent-wide, I'd try to visit on average one plant a week. This apparent diligence belies my native laziness; but you don't have to work if you're getting the grand tour. In the 1960s I was happy to spend two weeks at a crack living in a staff house at Upper Fraser or Oliver, B.C., or Rouyn-Noranda and trying to be useful, whether I was or not.

Somebody had to go out there and live on the site, because North-wood Mills started to go to rat-shit the minute we made our commitment. The old NFP mills hadn't yet hit bottom, and it took another $3-million worth of upgrades just to get them out of the ditch.

Dick Porritt was named president and CEO of Northwood Mills. I loved him dearly, but he was pretty much in the dark when it came to the forest industry. He was basically an old-fashioned miner — great on the hardware side of the business but not much interested in forest-related politics. He'd managed the Horne Mine, which was when he peaked, but I figured I could help him in the forests, and he was happy to have me do so. I guess I pushed myself forward, becoming the resident expert by default. Actually it defies all logic that Noranda stuck with Northwood through that first bad patch. I used to describe our actions by quoting Dr. Johnson's remark in reference to a man's second marriage: the triumph of hope over experience. But we kept on going, developed a game plan, and in the end built an entire industry where before there'd been none.

To simplify the story, I'll focus on the two mills up by Prince George, where Forestry Minister Ray Williston had laid out the pulp-harvesting area. The region was overripe for development. The Pacific Great Eastern railway ran south to Vancouver (and, as an instrument of provincial policy, was disposed to offer advantageous freight rates, so that we could overcome the obvious drawback of not being on the coast). Natural-gas pipelines were coming down from the north, and plenty of hydro was soon to be on tap, courtesy of the Peace River Power Development. Almost as important, Prince George had a far-sighted mayor, Garvin Dezell. He was all for progress, but not for the boom-and-bust cycle that had plagued other resource-dependent towns. To put a damper on land speculation, he bought and banked large tracts of undeveloped acreage, which were eventually released in carefully planned stages. So that was one less thing for Northwood to worry about: we wouldn't have to build ourselves a company town.

But we would have to build a pulp mill. We liked the look of a site about thirteen kilometres down the Fraser River, and we commissioned a feasibility study by John McCutcheon of the Foundation Engineering Company. He reported that the harvesting area we'd acquired would sustain a five-hundred-ton-per-day mill, estimated to cost about $68,000,000. So far, so good — but now we needed a partner. A year earlier we'd all been more or less old-fashioned miners. We needed someone who made pulp, consumed pulp, and produced paper, as well. All sorts of companies were approached, including Boise Cascade, Reed Paper, and Abitibi. We didn't talk with MacMillan Bloedel, who were dominant even at that time. They didn't like our incursion into the forestry business, and they had no use for the B.C. Interior. Reed led us up the garden path. They said they had no interest in the Prince George area, then turned around two weeks later and announced a partnership with Canfor, which became Prince George Pulp and Paper.

(But even this turned out all right in the end. Northwood launched a co-venture in 1968 with Prince George Pulp that resulted in a chemical plant to supply both our operations, bringing even more opportunities to the region. One of the people on their side of the fence at that time was Leopold Lionel Garrick "Poldi" Bentley, who'd changed his last name from Blockbauer after immigrating from Austria because he admired British automobiles. We became great friends. One day in early 1970 he met me at the Vancouver airport driving a rather sporty vehicle I'd never seen before. This was the BMW 2002, whose sterling qualities Poldi lauded to the skies, perhaps because he'd nailed down the western Canadian distribution rights and wanted to sell me one. What he eventually sold me on was the idea of going in with him to nail down the eastern Canadian distributorship, an arrangement that lasted for many years. Poldi, alas, died suddenly in 1989, and I think of our many travels together with sadness and affection.)

But I digress. In 1964 Noranda thought to approach the Mead

Corporation of Dayton, Ohio. Mead had long-standing ties to Canada, as investors in and sales agents for British Columbia Forest Products (BCFP). It was about the same size as Noranda but more diversified, operating sixty facilities in twenty-five states. We were expecting that they'd come in for at least seventy-five percent of any new project, based on their clout and expertise. But when I met with their then executive vice-president, Jim McSwiney, in New York, he said, "We're interested, but only if everything's fifty-fifty." That took us a while to wrap our minds around because we'd never gone halves with anyone. Ultimately we agreed and in 1965 Northwood Pulp was launched.

We hoped to have the pulp mill in operation by mid-1966 at a budgeted construction cost of $68-million. We later put hundreds of millions into its expansion, and to duplicate the complex today would run at least a billion dollars.

Our first stroke of bad luck came with the death of Keith Eadie, our vice-president and general manager, whom we'd hired away from MacMillan Bloedel. Eadie was killed, along with his wife and two other senior employees, when a disgruntled prospector blew their CP Air plane out of the sky. Eadie was a leader, someone we'd counted on to shepherd the project through. His death delayed our plans by months and would affect our subsequent performance for years.

Unfortunately, as is so often the case, the projected $68-million price tag soon began to escalate. McSwiney was zealously trying to hold the line, and Mead was bent on cutting back on anything they deemed nonessential. Theoretically Mead knew mills inside and out, which was more than I or anyone else at Noranda could claim. If they said we didn't really need this or that, I was in no position to argue. For example, we tried to get away without any holding tanks. That sounds pedestrian, but if you don't have tanks you have to shut down the entire operation if one unit breaks down — as it inevitably will. Every new plant is full of bugs, and there are thousands of components that can go off the rails. Our plant started up with no elasticity in the system; should anything untoward occur, there was nowhere to park the pulp while we got things back in order. Today the plant could boast about thirty-six hours' worth of elasticity. The day we opened, we couldn't have handled thirty-six seconds'.

That was a huge mistake. I don't fault Mead, but I question the consultants. Never hire a consultant who tells you what he thinks you want to hear. If Keith Eadie had been there, some of these problems would not have come to pass. They eventually got ironed out, but during the construction phase the contractors — and our project engineers in particular — allowed themselves to be steamrollered. Mead vice-president McSwiney, who became a great friend and showed great generosity, was a real dynamo, but he often was his own worst enemy. It was his way or a huge argument. Eventually he'd graciously accede to logic, but he intimidated people who knew more about the issue than he did. In turn, we might have been smarter, but at least it was a learning experience, and we wouldn't repeat the error of our ways.

Once the mill was up and running, we started to patch up the rest of our bag of bones. We acquired Eagle Lake Sawmills, ensuring that we'd have enough chips to supply over half the new pulp mill's requirements; we bought Bulkley Valley Forest Industries and Fichtner Lumber; and we built two identical sawmills down south, at Okanagan Falls and Princeton. But these were less than a rousing success, and we decided there was no future for us there. We didn't want to be just a lumber producer — we were striving to be fully integrated — so we eventually sold the mills to Weyerhauser. Before that, though, we moved in 1969 to pick up twenty-eight percent of British Columbia Forest Products, of which Mead already had a piece, together with Scott Paper. Eventually we became, along with Mead, the controlling shareholder of BCFP, a position that brought us into conflict with none other than Argus Corporation.

3

Takeovers – From Both Sides Now

British Columbia Forest Products, now known as Fletcher Challenge Canada, was largely the creation of the original Argus Corporation, which continued to hold about twenty percent of its shares. The main interest in the company was held jointly between our partners — the Mead Corporation and Scott Paper Company — through its joint venture, Brunswick Pulp and Paper. BCFP occupied a favourable position on the coast and owned a thriving pulp-and-paper mill at Crofton. Its guiding forces in the late 1960s were its president, Tom Beaupré, and his successor, Alec Hamilton, one of the best operators in the business.

Realizing that growth at their Crofton pulp mill was constrained by set timber limits, the company turned its attention to the northern Interior. It latched onto limits that had been originally assigned to Axel Wenner-Gren, a Swedish entrepreneur famous for his invention of the Electrolux vacuum cleaner. Wenner-Gren's ambitions had been foiled by a variety of circumstances, among them his ignorance of the industry, but the limits remained intact, and BCFP used them to develop a number of operations in the Mackenzie area.

Mackenzie today is the site of BCFP's modern kraft-pulp mill at the bottom end of Lake Williston, an artificial lake created by the Bennett Dam and the Peace River Power Development. The lake is named after the aforesaid Ray Williston. This site was only two hundred kilometres from Northwood's plant in Prince George. We believed that if Northwood and BCFP joined forces, the two companies acting in concert could form a much larger and more constructive force, and there would be productive synergies between them. Mead sold pulp for both, held a half-interest in Northwood, and owned about twenty-five percent of BCFP. A Noranda/Mead partnership acquisition of BCFP made sense, so we pursued it sensibly and wound up owning about sixty percent of the shares between us. This irked Argus Corporation, which wasn't accustomed to anyone challenging its authority or God-given right to run companies as it chose (even though it usually held minority positions). Noranda thus controlled the BCFP board and began to play an active part in the company's affairs.

By this time, however, BCFP's chairmanship had passed to Ian Barclay, a master corporate politician. The president was Ken Benson, a real tiger who usually found a way to achieve his ends. A mutually rewarding relationship developed between the two companies: BCFP processed Northwood's chips, Mead continued to sell both firms' pulp, and interchanges took place at the research level. But, as is so often the case, BCFP's management wanted to be (and to be seen to be) free of external influence and stood firm against any real integration. Against all odds, given its limited finances, the company made a success of the Mackenzie mill, then went on to develop a pulp mill at Saint-Félicien, Quebec, in partnership with the Donohue

Company and acquired the Blandin Paper Company in Minnesota. Finally, however, it overextended itself by paying far too much for the Elk River Timber limits on Vancouver Island. By then Northwood had pretty much decided to get out, which we did, in 1981.

By 1974 Noranda had concluded that Northwood was large enough in British Columbia, and that it was time to develop more broadly. We wanted to become more intregrated and international. The Noranda forest group (which was not until 1987 a separate company) started to look at other areas. We'd drawn up a list of desirable acquisitions, and on that list was the Fraser Companies, which owned pulp mills at Edmundston and Atholville, New Brunswick; a paper mill at Madawaska, Maine; and sawmills at Kedgwick and Plaster Rock, New Brunswick. The paper mill was more or less up to snuff, but the pulp mills had seen better days. The plus was that Fraser owned a huge and hugely valuable freehold acreage and held cutting rights to even more Crown land.

Fraser had four main shareholders, all of whom were getting on one another's nerves. Two great Nova Scotia families — the Jodreys, who own a good deal of downtown Halifax, and the Sobeys of grocery-store fame, who own the rest of the city — were open to offers. The third shareholder, Genstar (the Canadian firm that handles various Belgian investment funds), was prepared to sell and had made discreet overtures to Noranda's Ken Cork. This left the Crabtree family of Montreal, who owned the Wabasso textile mills. Conventional wisdom held that all four parties could never be persuaded to sell at the same time, under any circumstances, but Noranda was not deterred.

The Fraser deal was Noranda at its best. Those were halcyon days. We could afford Fraser and knew exactly how to get it. Ken Cork, Will Barbour (his assistant treasurer), Alf Powis, and I were in the forefront. Carl Frantz, the president of Northwood, played a part, too, as did Don Ford, the comptroller, and Warren Stubbington, the accounting manager. We worked together like a well-oiled machine.

41

First we went down one weekend to inspect the head-office operation in Edmundston, New Brunswick. The management people were
on our side; they'd had their fill of the owners' bickering and parsi-
mony. Fraser's president at that time was Kip Recor; Knut Grotterod
was his second in command. We all knew and liked each other.

After we'd confirmed the Jodreys' block and picked up Genstar's,
the Sobeys came on-side, but the obstacle remained the Crabtrees. I
went to see Roy Crabtree, then the chairman of Fraser, at his office
in Montreal. We'd never met before. I'd heard he was pleasant but
very much a loner. I said, "Mr. Crabtree, you should know that we're
making a bid for the Fraser shares tomorrow morning." He replied,
"Oh, you're the guys who bought the Genstar block. I guess we'd
better talk about the fishing camp."

I couldn't for the life of me figure out what he meant. It turned
out that Fraser had a marvellous fishing lodge up on the Kedgwick
River, where they would entertain their clients. It was a place
salmon fishers would kill for. This was the number-one thing on
Crabtree's mind because it was his major interest in the firm. He ran
the camp and hosted parties there. He could accept that we'd own
the company, but he wanted to remain majordomo of the camp,
which he did, until his retirement as director.

On the following Monday afternoon the Noranda executive
announced that we were about to bid on enough shares to give us
approximately fifty-one percent of Fraser's outstanding stock — a
total outlay of $35-million. The next morning, I got a call from my
good friend Harry Rosier, the president of Abitibi. He asked if he
could get in on the deal. When I told him it was not in the cards, he
rang off in bad humour, threatening to consult with his people about
countering our bid. About twenty minutes later I got word that we'd
gone over fifty percent, so I rang Rosier back. I said, "Forget it,
Harry. The deal is done." He chewed on that for a second and then
said, "What value did you put on the fishing camp?" I had a mole —
an old classmate of mine — at Abitibi who told me later that no one

could believe we'd pulled it off. Fraser was a natural building block for Noranda Forest: it was profitable, it was in the East, it was international, its paper mills needed Northwood's kind of pulp, and its sawmills might benefit from Northwood expertise. From Noranda's point of view, the whole arrangement couldn't have been better.

At first things worked out very well, but as time went on, Kip Recor, the Fraser president we'd inherited and supported, and I had a parting of the ways. He wanted to run the whole show from an office in Connecticut. His responses became increasingly perverse; no matter what Noranda suggested, whether it came through me or anyone else, he'd immediately do or say the opposite. Our relationship declined further when Noranda installed John Fisher as head of Fraser's strategic planning.

The Fraser experience lasted six years, from 1974 until 1980. Noranda spent a lot of money modernizing Fraser's pulp mills, which Lord knows needed it. Edmundston and Madawaska ate up $150-million, but what almost finished us off was Atholville, where we had to spend an extra $180-million — almost fifty percent more than we'd counted on.

But I thought this was the way to go, in part because we were extra-conscientious about New Brunswick. Richard Hatfield was premier, and we had dealt with him for many years. At the opening of the Atholville project, he talked about Noranda in glowing terms. He said that if there were a Nobel prize for companies, we ought to get it, and so on. I liked Hatfield. He was keen to get jobs for New Brunswick, but his taste in companies could be poor — witness the Bricklin-sports-car disaster. The province invested millions in a naive concept of building an automotive industry in the Maritimes. Everyone, from the scheme's promoter Malcolm Bricklin to the United Auto Workers, and doubtless countless lawyers in between, ate their lunch at the provincial trough. Hatfield was embarrassed but not destroyed. He liked Noranda because its jobs actually materialized and stayed put. Noranda asked for and got no favours, but our activities brought him votes. The company was at one time or another New Brunswick's second- or third-largest employer. Hatfield also viewed Noranda as a useful counterweight to the powerful Irving and McCain conglomerates.

In retrospect, though, we should have closed Atholville down and walked away. No amount of money could have saved it from the economy in the 1980s. We thought the retrofit would cost $125-million. Instead, we got hit with a construction workers' strike at a time when interest rates were bouncing around twenty-three per-cent. We sat there praying for an earthquake — but we didn't want to give up on the mill, for several reasons. One, it's hard to turn your back on an entire community; we'd have earned no points if we'd folded our tents and fled. Another, the mill had come complete with assigned timber limits, and we were sure another operator would immediately acquire them, thus complicating our plans and forcing us to look at alternative processing sites.

Make no mistake — if Noranda had walked away, some other company would have persuaded the provincial government to crank Atholville up again. That's the Canadian way. Some optimist comes out of the woods and says, "I can run it. Give me a $5-million grant," and away he goes. The mill or plant or mine or whatever struggles from day one, and more often than not the taxpayer keeps on prop-ping it up to save jobs and some politician's reputation. But you've got to hand it to these bottom feeders. They have a perfect sense of timing. They make the company that bails out look like a jerk for shutting down, and they play to the vulnerabilities of our elected representatives.

If I had to do it all over again, I'd bring in the wreckers. At the time, however, my judgment was clouded. I decided against Fraser's building a brand-new mill in Edmundston that would have done it all. I based my decision on the best advice at the time: we would get quality production from a rebuild at half the cost of a brand-new or "greenfield" project. If you do a quick run-through of all of Noranda's successes and failures, I think that the majority of failures stem from very personal choices. I (or whoever was in control) didn't pick the right person to do the job. Simply put, I took the wrong advice.

To get the job done, you have to delegate authority. If you try to hang on to all the strings, you'll tie yourself in knots. At some point you have to back off and trust that you've asked all the right questions. You have to recognize your own ignorance and make a judgment based on whether you believe the people you're talking to are knowledgeable and honest. A case in point was a guy hired to build Northwood's sawmills in the Okanagan. I thought at first that he was terrific, but I soon came to have the opposite view. To verify my suspicions, I called in someone else, who backed up the first guy, hoping he would effectively hang himself, which he did.

Good management comes down to people. You can go the last mile to ensure that a decision is technically and organizationally sound. You can run studies and hire consultants till you're blue in the face. You can pick the best people and let them do their thing. You can try to ask the hard questions, but you almost always get the same answer — the one your employees or consultants think you want to hear.

Northwood was a huge success because it had a solid foundation, financially and conceptually. Fraser was successful for a time, but we were hobbled by bad investment decisions. In the case of Northwood, one or two men were too dominant; in Fraser, one or two were too pliant, trying to be nice to everyone instead of making the necessary tough calls.

In both these cases, the decision-making processes were well defined and (by the book) correct. Owners, managers, and consultants were regularly and formally brought together to consider major decisions and review progress to date. Wrong calls were made only when and if they were based on faulty or inadequate advice.

Any process can be subverted if the wrong people control the levers. Looking back, Noranda's best decisions were those where collective judgment was applied. The notion of broadening the company's base may have started in the mind of John Bradfield or Alf Powis, but it immediately struck a responsive chord in directors of Noranda such as Bunny Foster, John Simpson, André Monast, and Jim Dudley. The senior executives of the company readily subscribed to the strategy. Once we'd targeted potential acquisitions, it wasn't long before they were established under the Noranda umbrella.

Regardless of how sound a decision-making process is, it can be confounded by the mixture and interplay of the various personalities working within it. But to have a well-thought-out process is vital. Its intrinsic checks and balances will ultimately reveal the deficiencies of the people who operate within it, and you can move to correct them.

So it was when Noranda (and many other firms) got caught in the inflation mentality of the late 1970s and early 1980s. The commonly held belief that things would never be cheaper, and that it was more economic to buy a company than to build one, led to a number of rash and inappropriate acquisitions. For its part, Noranda was driven to invest in manufacturing, mineral, and hydrocarbon concerns. Some of these investments would eventually result in well over a billion dollars in write-offs.

But there were plenty of good experiences, too. Because it started out as a mining company, Noranda was accustomed to what might be termed the takeover game. Mining properties were often discovered by people who didn't know much about developing or operating them, and who frequently didn't have sufficient capital. Thus they'd look to a major player who could provide the necessary technical expertise, along with infusions of cash. These activities weren't necessarily friendly. In the case of such highly promising discoveries as Quemont, Geco, or Hemlo, the corporate players would sit up and take notice — then rush in and try to take control. Noranda's virtue was that it knew what it was doing and was generally recognized as an attractive owner.

In the course of building Noranda Forest, beginning with

Northwood, our aim was clear. We wanted to be integrated right from the forest floor on up, we wanted to be national or even international in scope, and we wanted to produce the full spectrum of forest products, from lumber right on through to fine paper. To achieve this, we made strategic acquisitions along the way. The Fraser Companies and Maclaren Power and Paper, which we acquired in the early 1980s, were constructive investments from everybody's point of view. They needed us, we needed them, and we came to the venture with the necessary financial backing, together with technical and marketing expertise. This is the kind of takeover that works. Sometimes it's critical that the acquiror be vastly larger than the acquiree, but not always. More often the determining factor is that one firm has something the other needs and cannot itself provide. Takeovers conducted on this basis of course stand the best chance of panning out to the benefit of all concerned. Others are conducted in the name of hegemony, and while they may not prove to be all that constructive, they aren't necessarily doomed to failure. Lastly some takeovers are examples of corporate power run amok. These have never worked and never will.

In my experience it's usually desirable that a takeover be achieved either by the acquiror's offer of shares or other paper to the acquiree's shareholders, or by means of all-cash deals. But the all-cash deal can sometimes come complete with an Achilles' heel. All too often the cash has been originally provided to the acquiror by an ambitious bank, a fact that will cause financial pressures within the acquiring company when it has to pony up. What's even more likely to bring about serious problems down the road is the sheer ignorance of the acquiror's executives when it comes to the acquiree's business. This happens time and again; it's a sort of dead hand on the helm of Canadian business.

Several other takeovers in which I played a part as a director deserve some mention here. The first concerns Norcen Energy Resources Limited, the outgrowth of the merger of Northern and Central Natural Gas and Canadian Industrial Gas and Oil. It was a middle-rank firm, well respected, and distinguished by professional management. Its chairman, Ed Bovey, was an interesting man with a great passion for art and culture. As a result, the firm's offices were something of a gallery unto themselves. The board of Norcen was a lively mix of experienced people from Calgary, Winnipeg, Toronto, and Montreal. They were a collegial group with complementary skills and experience who worked well together. Norcen, at the time, was a very worthwhile enterprise that had done its share in developing Canada's resources and was continuing to do so.

One day in December 1979 Bovey got a call from none other than Conrad Black, who reported that he had just bought twenty percent of the company and wanted to have a chat. I was aware of Black's dominating tendencies as a shareholder, because he'd inherited a significant block of Noranda shares and had been in a prolonged tussle with Alf Powis over how he might exercise whatever power his shares conferred. Norcen called a board meeting to consider Black's intervention, and I urged Bovey that whatever Black had to say should be put in writing to guard against any future misunderstanding. Bovey went to see Black and was appropriately stroked by the offer of a seat on the Hollinger board. Black insisted that he was content with twenty percent of the company and proposed to name three directors only. All of which was reasonable — but things didn't work out that way. What Black was after (and got) was the ability to acquire a chunk of the M. A. Hannah Company of Cleveland, with which he was associated through Hollinger's involvement in the Labrador iron mines. As events transpired, Norcen's board was substantially changed, which was fair enough, but the new board (of which I was not a member) did not add any magic to the company's business. Eventually Hollinger's interest in Norcen was sold to Noranda where, on the evidence, the relationship has been constructive. This was a case of two takeovers — one by a company not in the business and another by a company in the business. The second one worked, in the sense of synergy at least.

The next example was the purchase in 1988 by Dofasco of Canadian Pacific's sixty-percent interest in Algoma Steel. At the time this seemed like a marriage made in heaven, at least as far as Dofasco was concerned. Algoma had long been recognized for its technological superiority in the manufacture of steel plate, rails, construction steel, and oil country tubular goods. Dofasco, for its part, was limited in its facilities and had been thinking about establishing a new mill — which would, however, have cost more than double the figure attached to the Algoma acquisition.

A committee of independent directors of Algoma (of which I was one) was assigned the task of assessing the fairness of the valuation of Algoma's assets; I was named to chair this exercise. With the professional advice of both Wood Gundy and Lancaster Financial, we were able to agree that the CPR was getting a fair price ($650-million) for its holding in Algoma.

So the deal was done, and at the time everyone, including the general public and financial analysts, believed it was great. Algoma was being acquired by a respected steel company, which in turn was getting assets it needed at one-half the cost of building a new plant. Sadly, no one assessed the potential wreckage to come from competing new technology and the actions of the Steelworkers Union at Algoma.

The new technology was the ability of mini-mills to make plate or sheet steel from scrap, which they were learning to do at much lower capital cost in electric arc furnaces than could be achieved in conventional mills. The union threat came from the hatred the Steelworkers had long borne Dofasco, which was a paternalistic union-free operation, unlike the strongly unionized Algoma. Moreover, the Steelworkers' locals at Inco in nearby Sudbury had just settled high, and that settlement became the yardstick for Algoma, according to tradition. A strike ensued at Algoma that cost in the hundreds of millions of dollars and effectively broke the company. Algoma was forced to take protection under the Company Creditors

Arrangement Act and made a deal (facilitated by Ontario's new NDP government) whereby the workers took a wage cut in return for shares and eliminated more than two thousand people from their own payroll. In the end Dofasco lost the company. The moral of the story: whoever you are, you better know what you are buying.

The purchase of Canada Packers by Hillsdown Holdings in 1990 came to a somewhat happier conclusion. Canada Packers was controlled by the McLean family of Toronto, who decided they wanted out. At this time Maple Leaf Mills, a separate entity, was already owned by Hillsdown, a major food-processing conglomerate based in Britain. Hillsdown, with a couple of other companies, shared dominance of the British market and had obtained a foothold in Europe, whence they were looking for a springboard to expand into North America. A marriage between Canada Packers and Maple Leaf Mills looked potentially rewarding; a committee of independent directors of Canada Packers was formed to assess the price being offered by Hillsdown and advise the shareholders of its fairness. As chairman of that committee, I ended up negotiating the deal with Sir Harry Solomon, Hillsdown's chairman. Solomon was and remains an effervescent and constructive acquisitor who had a vision for the new combination of Maple Leaf Mills and Canada Packers. Once this was in place, Solomon replaced both Bill McLean and the caretaker management of Canada Packers with his own people.

His managers moved quickly to reorganize a host of somewhat disparate businesses that dealt with everything from peanut butter to poultry. Maple Leaf Foods became Canada's largest food concern, but showed little prospect of dramatically increasing its profits. Eventually Hillsdown's management itself changed, Solomon left the chairmanship, and the company lost interest in its overseas acquisitions. Despite assurances to the contrary, Hillsdown summoned Maple Leaf Foods' board (of which I was a member) to a dinner meeting in Toronto and informed us a deal was in the works by which the firm would be sold to a company owned by Wallace McCain, who, although still a major owner of McCain Foods, had split with his co-owner brother, Harrison, and wanted to prove himself. A committee of independent directors assessed Maple Leaf Foods' valuation. It was agreed that McCain's offer was fair, and the deal went ahead.

The Algoma and Canada Packers cases were perfectly straight-forward. In both cases the takeovers took place for reasons of efficiency and hegemony; the second one at Maple Leaf was because Wallace McCain wanted to own his own food company and the own-ers wanted to sell. In both the incumbent president was replaced, but other than that, nobody came out much the worse for wear, and the companies' prospects remain as bright or dull as ever, depending on your point of view.

As this work is being concluded, an event has taken place that crystallizes many of the issues raised by takeovers of large corpora-tions: Hollinger's doubling of its twenty-percent interest in Southam through the purchase of its partner's interest. At the same time Conrad Black, the arrogant, fascinating, and cunning chairman of Hollinger, has announced his intention to bid for the balance of Southam shares and remove most of the directors who represent them.

Southam had long been a "family" company inasmuch as the Southam family have always owned the largest block of shares (as much as thirty percent in all) and the chief executive has always been a family member, several of whom were also on the board. While this condition prevailed, the quality, editorial freedom, and community responsibility of Southam's newspapers and other inter-ests were important aspects of corporate performance, which was not measured by profit alone, even though there was enough of that. Enough, but not as much as some of the competition.

In the spring of 1985 disaster struck when the competent, fifty-two-year-old president of Southam, Gordon Fisher, was found to have cancer of the liver and not long to live. In the period before a replacement could be identified, a corporate raider, generally believed to be George Mann of Unicorp, using the dealer services of

Gordon Capital and some financing from Hees-Edper, began to accumulate Southam stock with the probable objective of selling off parts of the company to pay for the whole. The Southam board chose to strive fiercely to maintain the company's independence.

A deal was struck between Southam and Torstar whereby each company exchanged their own shares for shares in the other, agreed to mutual board representation, cooperation in areas of common interest, and consultation regarding any subsequent sell-off of shares. By this means, Southam's continued independence seemed assured, and a newly found president could concentrate on running the business. That man proved to be John Fisher, the older brother of Gordon.

Southam then proceeded on a reckless course, making some bad acquisitions and failing to attend to profitability and to nurture the vital Torstar connection. The board became fractured to the point that eventually the holding in Torstar was sold, and a board/management shake-up ensued. The Southam family's holdings began to disperse and dissolve.

The long period of family domination was over, and the period from about 1987 to 1996 was not a happy one. Nevertheless, in due course a new president, Bill Ardell, was named, along with a new chairman, Ron Cliff, and life went on uneventfully until rather suddenly in 1992 Torstar sold its Southam holding to Hollinger.

The Southam board decided that, if a matching investor could be found by sale of new shares, a strong and independent ownership would remain, and the company would realize a welcome quarter-billion dollars in its treasury. The new shareholder was found in Power Corp., which then agreed with Hollinger that their preferred means of further growth in the publishing world in Canada would be Southam. In other words Southam would have first chance at any Canadian newspapers offered for sale. But that was not to be. Hollinger bought twenty-six Thomson papers in late 1995 and then fourteen Sifton papers in early 1996. Because there were Hollinger and Power directors on the Southam board, this gave rise to Southam's independent directors' preparing conflict-of-interest guidelines.

Hollinger and Power Corp. were now seriously at odds and convened to resolve their differences. Their private deal, into which they drew Southam's president, chairman, and treasurer, but not the board, was for Hollinger to exchange its Southam shares for ownership of Southam's small-town papers, which constituted about thirty percent of its business.

The independent directors of Southam took no time at all to reject this outrageous proposition, which would have meant selling off about one-third of the company's circulation and one-quarter of its profit without either consulting shareholders or seeking other buyers. The independent directors believed they had acted consistently from day one to preserve some independence for the company. As it turned out the management of the day, who acceded to the deal, was not up to the challenge, and the once independent family-owned Canadian corporation began its passage into history.

The next surprise was in March 1996, when Hollinger bought Power's twenty percent of Southam and announced an intention to bid for the rest. The independent directors were roundly criticized, primarily by Black himself, for making life difficult for Hollinger. That may be, but what you can say is that those directors, of which I had been one for twenty-six years, tried their best to prevent a cosy non-arm's-length, middle-of-the-night kind of deal.

My time as a director of Southam Inc. ended unceremoniously in July 1996 when Hollinger exercised its voting strength and removed the "obdurate rump" of independent directors. I concluded I would rather be one of those than the horse's ass who tried to insult us. I am certainly unashamed of my efforts over those years. Looking back on it we certainly had our highs and lows, although more the latter in recent years. I think one can conclude from this that, more than anything else, boards reflect their leadership's feelings. Southam's board had lots of brainpower but not a lot of tough business experience. With the tradition of everyone being heard, without strong direction, we thrashed around a lot and so got average performance. I hope the new united single control board will take the company up onto the sunlit uplands of greater prosperity.

The paradox underlying all these dealings was that Southam's dominant shareholders were acting primarily in their own interests, while the independent board members were trying to serve the interests of all shareholders. The dilemma was to decide which course was right from a business point of view, even though one was clearly the more proper.

To try to draw any eternal truths from the experience of takeovers is probably unproductive; like death and taxes, takeovers are an unavoidable part of business. Success comes to the person who buys — and sells — at the right price and at the right time. In a period of inflation such as was prevalent between 1975 and 1990, it was simply cheaper to buy a company than to build one. This strategy worked very well for many corporations, but it proved to be costly for certain holding companies and real estate operations. Although, I do believe that the best takeovers are those where the parties are basically in the same line or kind of business, the Algoma experience notwithstanding. Looking at the record, Power Corp., Olympia and York, Federal, Cancorp, CP, Brascan, and others have failed in or withdrawn from many earlier investments and now tend to be single-line. The same trend can be seen in other countries.

Finally, ego often plays a significant role in many takeovers, but these boardroom Machiavellis tend to forget a simple maxim: a stock doesn't know you own it.

This brings me to Brascan's determined and unhappy acquisition of Noranda.

4

Brascan's Opera Buffa

Those who subscribe to such theories might argue that my earlier experiences of corporate takeovers were directed by an unseen hand to prepare me for what was to come: the acquisition of Noranda Inc. by Brascan.

This unwelcome and unpleasant series of events spelled for me the beginning of the end of the company I'd helped to build. By 1986, when the dust had settled, Noranda as I'd known it was disappearing — but in a way, its passing was simply turnabout, even though fair play was at a premium. If you live by the sword, you're going to get stabbed in some portion of your anatomy sooner or later. Noranda had done its share of acquisition, so being the acquiree was perhaps only a matter of time and circumstance.

In 1979 Brascan, the former Brazilian Traction, Light and Power

Company Limited, foresaw the possibility that its South American holdings, which were facing hard times, were at risk of being nationalized. Therefore it sold its interests to the Brazilian government, cashing in to the tune of almost $450-million. This sale netted Brascan more money than it had immediate use for and made the company vulnerable to a takeover bid.

Brascan's then chairman was Jake Moore, whose life and career had roughly paralleled my own. He, too, was an alumnus of Ridley College, Royal Military College, and Clarkson Gordon. With the sale Moore had several options. He could have liquidated the company, gone in search of a suitable acquisition, or looked around for a partner. In December 1978, shortly before the sale of the Brazilian holdings took place, he started edging toward the third option.

On December 8, 1979, Moore approached Noranda president Alf Powis, in what Powis remembers as a somewhat "elliptical" manner, and raised the possibility of a merger. A quick study proved that, were Noranda and Brascan to join forces, they would form the sixth-largest corporation in the land, with assets totalling $3.4-billion. Better yet, the new entity would be eighty-five percent Canadian-owned and widely held. Noranda's executive committee was keen to pursue the project, and it looked sound to management. There hadn't been much in the way of a connection to date between the two firms, although we shared one director. But Noranda's management held a generally favourable opinion of Moore and the other Brascan executives, and the money was appealing in a period when Noranda had laid out a lot of cash on its various plants. Powis and I met with Moore, and I came away thinking that I couldn't imagine another two large companies getting together with so little in the way of problems.

We had proposed to Moore that we would offer one Noranda share, at $42, for two $19 Brascan shares. We'd also said that we would buy thirty percent of Brascan's shares on the open market. Moore wasn't averse to this, but said that $25 a Brascan share was more what he had in mind. Meanwhile, word of the deal had magically spread, and

Brascan's shares had jumped by more than $1.50 each. Powis backed off, telling the board that the merger was desirable but not worth reaching for.

Meanwhile, however, Moore had gone shopping in secret. Between his meetings with Powis and me, he'd aggressively pursued the idea of buying up retailer F. W. Woolworth. I believe he also gave thought to taking over Labatt. He was all over the map, but events conspired against the conclusion of his alternative plans.

By February 1979 everyone knew that something was in the wind. And so it was — in the form of the Edper Investments. Edper per se was a family trust that had enabled Peter and Edward Bronfman, the disenfranchised nephews of Sam Bronfman, to control Trizec Realty, a piece of the Continental Bank, the Montreal Forum, and, at one point, the Montreal Canadiens. The powers behind Edper were Trevor Eyton, a Toronto lawyer who'd handled some of Edper's previous acquisitions, and Jack Cockwell, a South African–born accountant who'd charted the course of the Bronfmans' investments.

Edper had been buying Brascan's shares ever since the previous December and by the end of February had accumulated a significant holding of 800,000 shares. On April 5 Eyton and Cockwell, along with Jaime Patino, a one-third partner in Edper Investments, informed Moore that they were about to make a bid for control of his company. Moore backpedalled, then hastened to persuade his board that they should press ahead with the Woolworth purchase. During this meeting a letter arrived, setting out Edper's offer of $27 a share for forty-five percent of Brascan's stock.

The fun went on for nearly three months. Edper formally announced its bid for Brascan; Brascan attempted to launch its own takeover bid for Woolworth. Frenzied activity took place on the trading floors of stock exchanges in Toronto, London, and New York, as well as in various courtrooms, when Brascan obtained an injunction against Edper, and Edper countered with a class-action suit against Brascan. On May 29, Moore realized that his shareholders were not going to be well served by a protracted battle for Woolworth, and that the $27 offer by Edper was generous, so he quit the battle. Edper got five million more shares than it was bidding for and thus ended up in clear control, with more than fifty percent of the shares in hand. Eyton was installed as Brascan's CEO and Cockwell as its senior vice-president in charge of planning.

We knew that Noranda would play some part in Edper's plans. Indeed, we'd always felt that if Brascan was nabbed by a predator we would be next on the list. Noranda was a great prize to whoever had the money, which Brascan did. Worse yet, we'd given Brascan a detailed appraisal of how the two companies would fit and work together. We'd really opened up the books; it amounted to full disclosure. When Edper took possession of the Brascan premises, they removed people swiftly. Eyton, Cockwell, et al. quickly obtained Noranda's master plan; there wasn't any time to burn the bridges or to turn on the shredding machine.

Our openness with Brascan left us in a doubly unenviable position and was a bad mistake on our part — though I've always felt that Moore had made a far worse blunder in not working with us. I wasn't Noranda's front man, being one of two executive vice-presidents at the time, but I often blame myself (and to a lesser degree, Powis) for not being more aggressive. In retrospect, we should have bought Brascan's stock. We had the financing more or less in place; we could have done in essence what the Bronfmans did. I think I could have influenced Powis and the board on such a deal. It would have been the right thing to do — good for most of both companies' holdings. For example, Noranda probably wouldn't have wanted to own Labatt or London Life. So we'd have kept the money from such liquidations and held on to Great Lakes Power and possibly a couple of peripheral mining interests. Otherwise, it would have been hands-off, business as usual on our part.

But not, as events would quickly prove, on Edper's.

Back in the mists of time a man named Noah Timmins had

received a block of shares in the original Noranda Mines. Timmins already had founded Hollinger Mines, which by 1978 was controlled by Argus Corporation, headed by Conrad Black. This block had come to number almost eight million shares — about twelve percent of the company.

In 1978 Black was giving thought to a takeover bid of his own and had shown signs of upping his stake in Noranda to twenty percent. He met with Powis in a series of legendary late-night encounters, the thrust of which was that we'd strike a standstill agreement, Black would take his place on the Noranda board, and the Argus shares would remain under his control. In February 1979 Black accepted Powis's proposal and promised to offer his shares to Noranda before he approached another buyer. Powis had made it clear that Noranda didn't wish to be taken over by Black or anybody else. As managers, we felt possessive. We had put a lot of ourselves into the company, the shareholders were happy, and we were operating profitably. In any event, Black's predatory instincts were forestalled. When he changed his mind and refused to join the board, Noranda issued enough treasury shares to take in the related mining companies Mattagami and Orchan and split Noranda's outstanding shares three for one, thus incidentally diluting Black's position and increasing shares of Noranda that were held by affiliated companies.

I believe that Black had no long-term interest in the resource industries. His real ambitions lay elsewhere, as witness his media holdings. Powis thought that Black had agreed to give Noranda first refusal if he wanted to sell his Noranda holdings. But Black went on to offer the Argus block first to Canadian Pacific and then to Brascan, which concluded the purchase (7.9 million shares at $21.50 each) in the first week of October 1979. Neither Powis nor anyone on the board or in management had an inkling of what was happening.

I thought that Black had behaved aggressively. He knew perfectly well of Noranda's interest in the Argus block. Black believes that only those who own their own companies are worth their salt, and refers to those who don't as "praetorians," harking back to the days of the Roman Empire, when he'd have been in his glory. At one point, when he and I were talking over dinner about the prospect of a takeover of Noranda, he argued that Noranda's management had no real claim to the company as they didn't own enough shares, which was debatable. He then told me precisely what my shareholding was at that time, confirming his reputation as a formidable corporate intelligence gatherer. It amounted to something over $1-million, which wasn't too shabby for a working guy.

So there went the Argus block. When Trevor Eyton called me on October 5 to break the news, I had the presence of mind to congratulate him on his choice of companies, but not much else, and told him I'd pass the word along. I was minding the store, because Powis was off in the middle of an Alberta gas field inspecting a Canadian Hunter operation. Powis called Eyton, who told him that Brascan's aims were to obtain between fifteen and twenty percent of Noranda's shares. Powis wasn't so sure that was all, and neither was I.

And so began a period during which Brascan spent every waking moment figuring out how they could get more and more of Noranda. By October 10 they'd picked up 1.6 million shares in addition to the eleven percent already held, and thus sat at about twelve percent, second only to the thirteen percent in the possession of Noranda-affiliated companies. The gap was narrowing with each passing week, and we knew where things were headed. To no one's surprise, on October 22 Eyton phoned with the news that Brascan had made yet another buy and now held over sixteen percent of the shares. A creeping takeover was under way.

In November 1979 Noranda decided to embark upon a rather complex takeover defence, the brainchild of treasurer Ken Cork. We issued an additional fourteen million treasury shares, some of which were bought by Zinor Holdings, a new entity owned by Frenswick Holdings (itself newly created), which was owned in turn by three different Noranda subsidiaries and affiliates. As a result, Noranda wound up with $266-million in cash, and Zinor exercised twenty-three percent control, as opposed to Brascan's (now diluted) fourteen percent. Eyton yelled at Powis, confirming our suspicion that Brascan was intent on becoming Noranda's largest shareholder with a view to taking an active part in our affairs. Powis, professing a desire to put an end to Eyton's misery, offered to buy Brascan out. Eyton yelled some more, and Powis went home, leaving Eyton to brood on the alleged but unproved impropriety of the Zinor transaction, to seek allies in his ongoing takeover scenario, and to draft a series of other demands that were subsequently rejected by the Noranda board.

Meanwhile in Quebec Maclaren Power and Paper was having trouble of its own. This firm had been established in the 1860s and had enjoyed a fair measure of prosperity ever since. Its pulp and newsprint mills at Buckingham and Thurso were small, efficient, profitable, and beautifully situated. It had its own power source, an assured wood supply, and easy access to major markets. But its owners, the Maclaren family, were split among themselves as to whether or not to quit the business and put their feet up in cushioned ease.

Tim Kenny, the firm's president (and later to be the first president of Noranda Forest), went looking for a buyer. Kenny is a born wise man — plugged-in, absolutely straight, and always a delight to work with. He was also a Maclaren on his mother's side. He sought the aid of the Montreal office of Wood Gundy, whose managing director, Mike Scott, was a lifelong friend of mine. Mike thought that, given the chance, Noranda would be more than interested in a deal and confirmed same in a call to me.

Other companies, including Canadian Pacific Investments and Domtar, were also eyeing Maclaren, but its management favoured Noranda. They liked and trusted us; our reputation was good. When I went to see Yves Bérubé (who eventually came to the Noranda Forest board), then forestry minister in René Lévesque's government, he said, "We always knew that Maclaren was going to go to one of the big companies, and Noranda is the least worst." That may sound like faint praise, but in fact it shows the esteem in which we were held.

And so in January 1980 we struck a $240-million deal, with payment in Noranda treasury shares. That arrangement suited both parties, particularly as it enabled a tax-free rollover for Maclaren shareholders, but it annoyed Brascan. Naturally they saw the purchase as yet another attempt to further dilute their position, which it did. But we'd been prepared to make the buy for years and would have gone ahead, anyway, even if Brascan hadn't been in the wings. Eventually even Trevor Eyton had to admit that Maclaren was an excellent company to have and to hold.

Things were quiet until March 1981, when Noranda moved to acquire MacMillan Bloedel. From that point forward, Brascan had come to believe that they must get Noranda if not now then pretty soon.

At this time Noranda Forest didn't exist as a separate company; it was simply Noranda's forest division, which division owned Northwood Mills, Fraser, Maclaren, and, in partnership with the Mead Corporation, Northwood Pulp and Timber and a slightly more than controlling interest in British Columbia Forest Products. This last had been a good thing while it lasted, but we knew the arrangement was winding down. Our interest in BCFP didn't allow us to exercise any real control, and we felt we could get along without it. On the other hand, we'd always known that if the opportunity arose we'd be eager to buy MacMillan Bloedel.

MB had long been vulnerable and the object of many and varied takeover affections. Back in 1978 Argus Corp., which held a seventeen percent share in Domtar, decided to offer this holding to MacMillan Bloedel. Upon learning this, Domtar said it would itself go after MacMillan Bloedel. MacMillan Bloedel, having bought Argus's shares, expressed its intention of going after Domtar. These pyrotechnics excited Canadian Pacific Investments, which thought it, too, might take a run at MacMillan Bloedel. Premier Bill Bennett, unimpressed by all the millings-around, declared that B.C. was not for sale and sent everybody back to their respective corners.

And there the matter rested — at least, until February 1981, when I was sitting in a board meeting and a message arrived saying that Teck Corp. was prepared to offer its approximately eight-percent holding in MacMillan Bloedel for a good price, something in the realm of $40-million. This was manna from heaven; it gave us a stepping stone. I went into high gear and made a pitch to the board. Fortunately our long-term strategic-planning process had prepared everyone for this eventuality, and fifteen minutes later we'd agreed to buy the shares.

Meanwhile, however, the British Columbia Resources Investment Company (BCRIC), a creature of the provincial government, had picked up about twenty percent of MacMillan Bloedel's shares. In March 1981 BCRIC made an offer for an additional twenty-nine percent, which would have frozen Noranda out. I was on the phone immediately to Cal Knudsen, who then headed MacMillan Bloedel. Cal is an American, who learned his trade with George Weyerhauser in the States. At first glance he seemed to be the typical branch-plant manager, content with transposing the techniques that had worked elsewhere. He'd been chairman for five years and had no great liking for BCRIC, which was run by MacMillan Bloedel's former president, Bruce Howe. Both Knudsen and I felt that BCRIC was a very unsuccessful and unproved company; nobody wanted to be bought by it. Also, the government had by this time changed hands, and the Social Credit premier, Bill Bennett, felt no obligation to support his predecessor's creation.

I called Knudsen on a Friday, told him that we now had a significant interest in his company, and asked to visit him. We arranged to have lunch on Sunday. I flew out that morning and back that night. Knudsen was absolutely marvellous. He and his wife, Julia Lee, received me at their home. Despite the purpose of my visit, they treated me with the greatest kindness and openness. That's when I quickly began to reevaluate my opinion of the man. He was totally objective and nonconfrontational. He didn't like the idea of a takeover of MacMillan Bloedel and said so, but he admitted that it was inevitable, and that he was therefore going to have to make it work as well as he could. I think he preferred Noranda over other possible acquisitors.

So the deal was in motion. I met with Premier Bennett, who said that he didn't want to see an overconcentration in the industry, but that he also didn't wish to regulate it to death. He'd been opposed to the earlier Canadian Pacific bid because it seemed at odds with government policy. I offered to divest Noranda of its share in British Columbia Forest Products (as we had always intended to do from the beginning of the MB caper). Bennett didn't demand this, although he asked that we attempt to sell to a corporation that was itself owned in large part by B.C. interests, and that we confine ourselves to a fifty-percent share of MacMillan Bloedel. He knew that we'd been good shareholders of BCFP, and our willingness to sell out was another mark in our favour. And so, after a brief attempt by BCRIC to top our offer, we acquired 49.9 percent of Macmillan Bloedel in a cash-and-share bid totalling $626.5-million. This was, for its time, the largest takeover in Canadian history — although we held the record for only about a week.

In order to make the deal, we had to issue convertible preferred shares, which potentially further diluted Brascan's position in Noranda. When questioned by a business reporter whether Noranda was now bullet-proof to takeover, Powis replied that his prime motivation had been to serve the shareholders, and that nobody was bullet-proof unless they owned fifty-one percent of the company. Events would prove him right.

At the outset Noranda brought five directors to the MB board, who together represented more than one hundred years of experience in the forest industry. Some of the MacMillan Bloedel people resented the Noranda directors, but they were wrong to do so. MB had the best forest base in Canada, which is why, whenever you see an antilogging protest on television, it's bound to be one of their holdings. The company was founded by a forester, who'd staked out all the finest B.C. coastal timber. Yet MB weren't doing nearly as well with it as they could. Their head-office apparatus was unwieldy and impenetrable. They had a number of questionable capital projects looming. Thanks to Knudsen's generosity and fair dealing — he brought me into all MB's deliberations — I got to know the company almost at once and worked hard to make sure I knew where it was going.

As an amusing sidelight, Trevor Eyton, having objected at first to Noranda's MB acquisition, invited himself onto the MacMillan Bloedel board. Brascan thereafter referred to MB in a highly posses-sive way.

MB's president was at this time none other than Ray Smith, last heard from calling me names aboard an airplane. He was leery of people from Toronto and viewed his new major shareholder with a great deal of suspicion. I respected his talents; he did well during a difficult time when few options were open to him. He was an excel-lent housekeeping leader, but not an originator or a visionary. After a while even the best housekeepers tend to become overly conserva-tive and stop at top dead centre.

But there were hard decisions to be made by Knudsen and Smith. In 1981 the company ran an operating loss of $26-million and change. The stock dropped from $62 at the time of the takeover to $22. The *Wall Street Journal* termed Noranda's acquisition one of the biggest blunders in Canadian history.

Compared with Noranda, MacMillan Bloedel's head office was top heavy beyond belief. They had vice-presidents for everything. I said to Knudsen, "You've got eighteen hundred people. Noranda has only three hundred. Surely there are efficiencies possible." MacMillan Bloedel's first response was to call in McKinsey and

Company, a management-consulting firm. They sent over one of their senior operatives, who talked about examining our asset base, which would help us decide what business we were in. I said to him, "You can't really think we didn't know what business we paid over half a billion for. Don't hold your breath — we're going ahead with what we know."

Instead, Knudsen, Smith, and I convened a meeting of twenty-odd MB executives and operational managers, and locked them up in Vancouver's Hotel Georgia. Then we asked them what they thought we ought to do. Not to my surprise, this worked. We came out after two days with a unanimous plan to reorganize along regional and divisional lines, cut out head-office redundancies, and get on with the job. It's amazing how quickly the task was done. When you've got to lay on this sort of massive reorganization, imposing it from above does no good. People have to believe, first of all, that it's right, and second, that it's their idea. The result was that the managers achieved a great deal more independence and ran things better than before.

Eventually, in spite of his support for revamping the company, Knudsen seemed to lose interest in it. He told me he hadn't come north to run somebody else's shop — that Noranda was bad enough, and that, coupled with the looming shadow of Brascan, things looked better back where he'd started from. He returned to the States and became a sort of corporate dilettante, spending time on a number of American boards and at his vineyard in Oregon.

I'm sorry I rained on his parade, and I hope he bears me no lasting ill feelings. I know that I was the face of the new owner; as the chairman of the board, I was inevitably the guy who was buttonholed by the media or by shareholders. In fact the company once conducted a survey asking people who they thought ran the place. Knudsen came in second; Ray Smith, who in fact was in charge, came third; and yours truly, the guy from Toronto, topped the list. I suppose that MacMillan Bloedel believe that their fate would have been different, perhaps better, if Noranda hadn't come calling. We'll never know. But whatever happened and however anybody views it, Noranda was probably a better bet than BCRIC would have been.

Meanwhile, out in the world, the economy tanked, and Noranda had a real tough time. We built some mills, but that was about it. We weathered a strike that never should have happened and laid off hundreds of people; for quite a long time we cut back on everything that moved. We also limited MacMillan Bloedel's issuance of common stock to avoid diluting our position, although they met their financing needs by issuing preferred shares.

As we struggled on into the 1990s, it became clear we'd always be limited to fifty percent of MB because of public policy in B.C. The B.C. coastal forest was going to be forever dogged by environmentalists and native land claims, not to mention cash-strapped governments. Our ownership had, so to speak, put us on the map — a prize company owned by a newly created forest enterprise added to Noranda's mystique. We'd done all right by it, but by 1991 our finances were stretched after years of depressed forest-product markets; the MB investment increasingly looked better in cash than in shares. So, on my own, but reflecting the consensus view of Noranda Forest management, I recommended to our board that we consider selling. Brascan (which by then controlled Noranda), in the person of Jack Cockwell, rejected the idea quite strongly at the time; however, two years later, a broker came calling and suggested that the MB shares could be sold. Which we did — at the wrong time in the market and against my advice at that time. If we'd waited three months, we would have booked a good profit over the ownership period. As it was, we broke even. So at least the *Wall Street Journal* article was wrong!

I believe that Noranda was a constructive influence on MacMillan Bloedel. We never pushed them into things they didn't wish to do. We weren't interventionist; we tried to get the company organized in an efficient and rational way and to make sure people had the authority to do the best they could, which is my prescription for good management under any circumstances. We supported management all the way. But our best, which I think we gave, wasn't enough to make good profits in bad times.

Returning to the Brascan/Noranda saga . . . In July 1981 Brascan made an unlikely alliance with the Caisse de dépôt et de placement du Québec, a provincial government agency that administered, among other things, the government's $14-billion pension plan. The Caisse had been a Noranda shareholder for quite some time. Together, its and Brascan's holdings totalled almost 25 million common shares — 21.5 percent of the total, as opposed to the 21.1 percent held by Zinor. A new entity, Brascade Resources, was created, owned seventy percent by Brascan, thirty percent by the Caisse. Everyone at Noranda saw the light of a rapidly approaching train.

Parti Québécois Finance Minister Jacques Parizeau was in the thick of these events. The Caisse had been his bright idea back in 1965 when Jean Lesage was premier. Paul Desmarais of Power Corp. believes that Parizeau conceptualized the Brascade deal with Conrad Black to enable Black to sell his shares for enough cash to finance the acquisition of Norcen and Hannah, thinking it would be in Quebec's best interest. If true, the Brascade-deal structure, which ultimately worked for Brascan, might have been co-authored by Conrad Black. Thus is another legend born!

The Brascan–Caisse alliance was both peculiar and unprecedented. If the Caisse themselves had bought up a controlling interest in Noranda, that would have been strange enough — although they liked to become a proactive shareholder, as they are in Domtar. But to participate in a minority way with another company was very odd and, as things turned out, a very costly investment, because the Caisse lost a ton of money over the years.

In late July Brascade announced that they would attempt to pick up another 20 million common shares of Noranda, along with 1.8 million preferred shares, for a total outlay of $921-million. If they did so, they would gain forty-percent control. They had meanwhile exceeded the twenty-percent plateau by purchasing an additional 5.5 million shares in June.

Noranda pondered its options and rumours flew. Even this late in the day, there were still several possible lines of defence, among them, a merger with Gulf Canada or a share exchange with Dome Petrolcum. These and other options bit the dust because they offered no real benefit to the shareholders. A meeting of Noranda executives with Parizeau in early August produced little more than Parizeau's statement that he had no right to run the Caisse; he could just ask questions. After delivering himself of this homily, Parizeau began to laugh, so pleased was he with his little joke and with three anglo executives (Powis, Cork, and Bill James, an executive vice-president) coming to him, caps in hand. Nor did other Caisse executives feel inclined to deviate from their course.

And so, on August 13, 1981, Powis, recognizing that the tide could not be held back and that it was better to have the money in the till than on the street, almost single-handedly extracted from Brascade the price of $40 each for 12.5 million treasury shares. Brascade would now dominate Noranda with a thirty-seven-percent equity and six seats on the sixteen-man board. Top to bottom, the victory had cost Brascan a total of $1.9-billion.

That month, Noranda lost money for the first time in its history. A year and a half later, the stock for which Brascan had avidly shelled out $40 was down to $12.

As the months passed, my mood changed toward our Brascan masters. I'd very quickly realized that these guys weren't going to be passive owners, and I anticipated the worst of the worst.

Powis was always the leader and front man for Noranda, although Bill James and I were the lieutenants and had a lot to say. After the knockout blow of August 1981 he remained the boss. (Only Bill James had the wit to move on to better things.) On the other side of the fence were Trevor Eyton and Jack Cockwell, jokingly referred to in Noranda circles as the Enforcer and the Ayatollah. They were driven men whose experience and goals were completely different from those of the Noranda people they replaced or overshadowed. Cockwell was the quintessential backroom guru who spent every waking hour concocting arcane financial mazes, which led eventually to the control of about one-quarter of the TSE's share values. He would stride into a room, shake hands all round, and remove his jacket before sitting down. He reminded me of a boxer entering the ring to slug it out with his opponent — perhaps because he has cauliflower ears. He struck me always as one-dimensional, though a genius in his fashion.

Eyton, on the other hand, is a big shambling man, a former Varsity Blue lineman, who brimmed with confidence, cunning, and connections. He was frequently late for meetings, and whiled them away by scribbling comments in a small notebook he always carried with him. Some viewed him as a sort of corporate bouncer (hence, the Enforcer tag) whose primary role was to muscle people into line with the aspirations of Brascan. Witness Noranda's adoption of the Brascan salary scheme. He wanted his way at any cost, but he wanted also to be loved by the world at large.

Attempts to achieve this were Brascan's Christmas and pre-annual-meeting parties notable primarily for their guest lists. They were top heavy with such luminaries as the Reichmans, assorted bank presidents, senators, corporate bosses, and selected investment dealers, many of whom seemed to attend out of a painful sense of duty. Tables were beautifully set, and people were seated with inordinate care to ensure that those who ought to rub shoulders did. I always felt like the captured Argentine naval captain paraded in full-dress uniform during the surrender ceremony on the deck of the conquering British warship during the Falklands War — or perhaps like a prisoner at a Roman triumph. The executives of Brascan's previously independent companies (Peter Widdrington of Labatt, Earl Orser of London Life, Hart MacDougall of Royal Trust, Ken Field of Bramalea, and Harold Milavsky of Trizec) seemed to share my discomfort.

But even Brascan's nominal bosses were on display. On cue, Eyton would rise and deliver one of his patented speeches, then present a gift of some description, like a trip to Hawaii, to a suitably aston- ished Peter Bronfman. Strangely enough, Edward Bronfman never got the same degree of fawning attention, even though he, too, was always present. Peter Bronfman retained Eyton as an apparently trusted lieutenant, but it was Cockwell, the real boss, who ruled the Brascan roost, because he and his coterie of financial engineers knew all the numbers.

Eyton and Cockwell professed to value Noranda highly, but they did little to encourage the people who'd made it a success. They didn't know our business yet I was seldom consulted, and I wasn't alone. Cockwell was pleasant when things were running smoothly, but wasn't inclined to discuss matters with anyone.

When times got tough, the tough got going in several different ways. Commodity prices plunged in unison. When first on the Noranda scene, Eyton remarked to the press that he didn't believe Noranda should be "vulnerable to the ups and downs of the mining industry," and added that "within two or three years, we should be able to impress our strategy on the company." No one knew exactly how he hoped to single-handedly disregard the market, and no one wanted to ask.

In any event, Bill James left to run Falconbridge and I was named Noranda's president and chief operating officer in April 1982, giving me the unfortunate distinction of presiding over the first loss in Noranda's history. At least, at $83-million, its dimensions were impressive.

Unimpressed by red ink, the unions responded with their usual common sense and indulged in several crippling strikes. Outside analysts and other armchair quarterbacks demanded draconian gestures — perhaps firing the entire head office and moving to a basement on Eglinton Avenue in Toronto. The reality, however, was that Noranda had little fat to cut, a story we had trouble getting across to the media and to the financial community. I suppose we should have, as was debated, sold the corporate airplane for the "optics" only, but we needed it and would have been reduced to sneaking out the back door and chartering one. We committed ourselves to the Hemlo gold mine, the great discovery in northern Ontario. While this was a step forward, we took two steps back when we were finally forced to deal with a number of highly questionable mining properties, which would eventually require write-offs approaching $1-billion.

Not surprisingly it wasn't long before Brascan began to doubt the wisdom of its acquisition. It responded to criticism from the Caisse and took to calling monthly breakfast meetings at Toronto's King Edward Hotel. Powis and I attended with Eyton, Cockwell, Denis Giroux and Pierre Lamy (two of the Caisse directors), and a token nonaligned neutral party in the person of Bill Wilder, who was on our executive committee. The meetings were done outside the board and flew in the face of good management or proper corporate governance. I've never understood why the board went along with it. A full executive committee meeting every month would have sufficed. Everything would have been open and minuted. As it was, the breakfasts engendered only bad feeling and distrust.

These private meetings also gave Eyton and Cockwell the chance to test-fly the Brascan Creed — a statement of corporate purpose that was supposed to be adopted and promoted by all their companies. It started off by saying that Brascan reserved the right to make senior personnel appointments, that it wouldn't seek to dominate boards, that dividends would be paid to common shareholders even in years when the company ran a loss, and so on. (Between 1982 and 1993, Noranda paid out $3-billion in dividends, meanwhile reporting only $1-billion in profits.) All senior officers were forced to receive a substantial portion of their salary package in the form of allocated shares. These were supposed to skyrocket in value and make us rich. An added burden was the debt one had to assume. Unfortunately Brascan ignored the fact that they were running capital-intensive companies in cyclical industries.

Meanwhile, Noranda had not remained static. It had always been a difficult company to handle in terms of management structure and seemed to require a restructuring every five years or so. It had occurred to Powis and me that perhaps the greatest shareholder value would be derived from carving the whole thing into sensible units and taking them public, retaining perhaps a twenty-percent interest. What we arrived at involved, as a first step, a split between forestry and mining operations. Brascan was happy to see the proceeds of the sale of twenty percent of Noranda Forest in the till. When we were through, Powis and I looked at each other and agreed that, if the scheme was put into practice, there weren't going to be jobs for both of us.

So it was that I moved to form Noranda Forest. The shift was unceremonious, but the task of taking Noranda Forest public, which I greatly enjoyed, made it acceptable. The creation of Noranda Forest was the largest initial public offering in Canadian history at the time; I thought of it as the logical culmination of long effort and the company-building process. And I was lucky to get out of the line of fire. I had a nice soft landing — like being tossed into a haystack from a high-speed auto accident.

One moral of the Noranda/Brascan tale is that unless the top company owns all of a subsidiary, they're probably better off out of it. Very few holding companies know how to hold companies. In that sense, Brascan is merely the most conspicuous example of how these catchall conglomerates exist primarily to gratify their owners' egos. The financial realities are that you should own one hundred percent of the assets you're managing and put them to the best use you see fit. If you know what you're doing, you'll be all right. If you don't, you'll be out of a job.

I've given some thought to the question of whether some companies are unmanageable — just as Canada is frequently judged to be ungovernable. Size is a factor, no doubt about it, but some businesses have to be big, so their managers must learn how to run them. But no big business runs as efficiently as an efficient small business. The notion that a good manager can run anything is likewise question-able; you're best at minding your own store. Get too many strings in your bow and you won't know the players, the plants, the processes, or the competition. You can go to a certain point of understanding, but beyond, the path gets steep and slippery. That's why financial gurus like the Brascan executives don't necessarily make good owners of industrial corporations. Nor does General Motors necessarily make a good owner of a computer company. The big-time owners of the 1970s and 1980s have largely been and gone. Argus Corporation was once a name to be feared, which has now been substituted by Hollinger and is solely in the publishing business. The once great Canadian Pacific has had a run of bad news. Brascan itself had to have been a fair disaster. In the recession of the early 1990s it was close to the wall, but the banks didn't dare call, because they'd bring the house down around everybody's ears.

Other catch-all conglomerates certainly don't seem to have a lasting quality. You can search the files and turn up few examples of success. I think of Canadian Corporate Management, the group put together by Clarkson Gordon's senior partners ostensibly to lead their clients out of the estate-tax woods by purchasing their private companies. This was a nice tidy insiders' pastime while it lasted, but it disintegrated in the end, as did countless others such as Federal Industries, Genstar, BCRIC, and Olympia and York. The only hold-ing tanks that seem to endure are the oil companies and some of the mineral concerns — but they're involved in essentially one industry worldwide and can bring their expertise in development, as well as bags of money, to the party.

With the mellowness of hindsight, I have come to view the Brascan episode as a sort of comic opera. I told people at the time, and still believe, that the old Noranda Inc. was dead in all but name in 1986 when we split off Noranda Forest, and Brascan appointed the president of Noranda Inc. But like any good opera, there were still a couple of plot lines to resolve. Powis and I were told that we'd be chairmen (of Noranda and Noranda Forest respectively) for life — that we could stay put, as long as we had our wits about us and didn't walk down the street shaking bottles at passersby. That was nice, but I didn't take it to the bank. I'd always thought I might hang around for two or three years at the most after I turned sixty-five. In fact Brascan wanted me gone after only a year and a half, and they dumped Powis before he became a pensioner.

Well, that was then, and there's nothing to be gained from Brascan-bashing. Noranda had a good long run, as did I. What, after all, is a company? It's a collection of assets and a corps of people who learn to get along with one another and join in some constructive purpose. Noranda built plants and mills and mines, not to mention communities where before there'd been none. Prince George, which formerly creaked along with its wooden sidewalks and hotels, is now the home of the University of Northern British Columbia. New Madrid, Missouri, now has the industrial base of Noranda Aluminum to balance the local farm economy, and Hemlo has added stability to the Marathon-Manitouwadge area of northwestern Ontario. I later had the great satisfaction of attending a Senate hearing at which one of the senators praised what we'd done for British Columbia.

Noranda came and it went. It would have been nice if things had turned out differently, if we could have preserved Noranda's independence; but they didn't and we couldn't. But nothing can take away the fact that it was great fun while it lasted.

5

| Softwood Hardball

Hardball is America's national game. They've been playing it for years, and they're very good at it. They're happy when a contest goes into extra innings; they never give up, and if the calls aren't going their way, they demand a change of umpires. Then, if that doesn't work in their favour, they demand a replay.

The Americans play hardball when it comes to international trade. The home team's record is the only thing on their minds. After all, the visitors don't vote in U.S. elections. As long as the Yanks walk away a winner, everything's fine and dandy. If not, watch out — they'll get you next season no matter what. That's the way they are, the way they've always been. Canadians' failure to recognize this fact (and where were those scouting reports when we needed them?) has given rise to any number of lopsided contests.

Chief among these, from my point of view, was the bitter dispute over softwood lumber, which dragged on throughout the 1980s and continues right up to the present day. This highly acrimonious and seemingly endless battle saw me emerge for a period as a "leader" of the Canadian forces — a responsibility that added a challenging side dish to my already full corporate plate.

The nub of the conflict was as follows. A portion of the American lumber industry and a fair number of American politicians indulged in acts of outrageous protectionism, bolstered by highly spurious arguments and the selective use of dubious "facts" and figures. Closer to home, our own governments, both federal and provincial, were willing to turn their backs on the nation's most important industry to swell their coffers and continue a lockstep march toward the implementation of a dubious grand design — free trade with the U.S.

In the course of these events, Canadians learned once and for all that our forest industry was more fragile and fragmented than was good for it. The industry was attacked by American policy and would have done well to respond as a cohesive body. But at the time we were almost totally disorganized. Nobody had to bother dividing us to effect a conquest. Our problem was to create, on short notice, a unified defence.

Chances are, the details of the softwood-lumber dispute have faded from your mind, if they ever lodged there in the first place. Perhaps you'll recall only that Canada and the U.S. seemed to be on the verge of armed hostilities over "shakes and shingles," which sounds more like a disease than a trade dispute. But we'd do well to examine the issues at length, because what befell the forest industry isn't a long-gone entry in the record books. The Americans are still there, ready to send the heart of their batting order up to the plate again.

Softwood lumber is lumber cut from spruce, pine, and fir trees. A consumer goes to the lumberyard and buys it in the form of two-by-fours and other stock sizes to build a house, deck, shelving, or picket fence. Cedar shakes and shingles go on your roof.

How much lumber are we talking about? A great deal. Canada is the world's third-largest softwood producer, exceeded only by the U.S. and the former Soviet Union. But we are by far the world's largest exporter, shipping over thirteen billion board feet (valued at approximately $4.2-billion) to the U.S. alone in 1992. In 1991 our softwood industry employed directly at least sixty thousand people, plus many thousands more when secondary spin-offs and ripple effects are considered.

About two-thirds of Canadian softwood lumber comes from British Columbia, which like other provinces has what's called a stumpage system. This system allows a private company such as Noranda Forest to cut timber on Crown land, subject to the payment of certain fees and the fulfilment of other obligations such as reforestation, fire protection, and road-building. Ninety percent of Canada's forests are owned by the provinces (in the form of national parks) or by the federal government, and forestry is a provincial responsibility. Thus the forest industry must deal with eleven separate jurisdictions, all of which set terms, conditions, and stumpage formulae of their own.

The important thing to bear in mind is that, when it comes to working out stumpage payments, a tree is deemed to have no value unless and until it can be converted to a profitable end product. This concept has been taken out of context by forest-industry critics and rephrased as, "Zimmerman says trees worthless until they are cut down." But no one knows what a tree will bring until it, or whatever is made from it, is sold. The economic (as opposed to environmental, spiritual, or scenic) value of a single tree — or, by extension, of a province's standing timber — is therefore its selling price, minus whatever it costs to cut, transport, and mill the tree, then ship the resulting products to their final destinations. The provinces, as landlords, get the stumpage fees. The forest companies, as tenants, get the profits, if any. Stumpage fees are also supposed to support a given province's forestry service and to fulfil legislated silvicultural requirements — in other words, to make sure that enough new trees are planted to replace those that are cut.

B.C.'s stumpage system was based on a formula that related to market prices in the preceding fiscal quarter. If the market went up, so did the stumpage fees. If it went down, they were adjusted to suit. Quebec and Ontario, the other major softwood producers, had systems that weren't quite so market-sensitive but were nevertheless fine-tuned from time to time.

By contrast, something approaching half of all American commercial timber is owned by private companies. These companies are not a strong part of the softwood dispute; they harvest their own land and don't pay stumpage to anybody. The other fifty-plus percent, however, is purchased from state and federal forest authorities by means of auctions, at which the companies make bids based on their best estimates of what markets will be like in the future. To do this with anything approaching accuracy demands a degree of prescience denied to ordinary mortals.

This practice of auctioning timber was the genesis of the softwood dispute. In 1979 and 1980, when everything looked rosy, the Americans made vastly extravagant bids, to which they were committed three to five years down the road. These bids proved ruinous when prices declined by up to fifty percent as the recession of the early 1980s hit. By 1982 U.S. firms were paying a great deal more for their trees than Canadians or anyone else. By 1984 they were in such bad shape that Congress attempted to bail them out by passing special relief legislation. This situation, I repeat, was their own fault — or rather the fault of the system under which they operated.

A downturn in the American producers' fortunes had become apparent even earlier on. In 1981 the state of Oregon convened a panel that attempted to pin the blame on, among other factors, "unfair subsidies" conferred on the Canadian forest industry by our provincial governments. Led by Senator Bob Packwood and Congressman James Weaver, and with funding provided by three major firms located in the Pacific Northwest, the Americans claimed that Canada had succeeded in snatching nearly one-third of the entire U.S. softwood market because Canadian producers paid less for their trees than their American counterparts. At the time we did in some cases pay less, but it certainly wasn't the result of connivance with government; it was because our system was more market-sensitive. It was also a fact that the delivered cost of comparable logs to sawmills in both countries was roughly the same. According to Packwood's claim, however, the difference between Canadian and American stumpage rates was in and of itself a subsidy. The U.S. Department of Commerce was asked, for the first but not the last time, to impose a countervailing duty against Canadian softwood imports.

This approach conveniently ignored a long-held international trading rule that sovereign countries price their own natural resources at will. No one suggested, for example, that American petroleum products should be barred at the border because Texas oil royalties were less than those levied in Alberta. Or that U.S. metal producers, who also benefited from more favourable royalty rules than Canadians, were competing unfairly. Or that Canadian electricity exports should be taxed because riparian rights (for water used in the production of hydroelectric power) were less costly than the coal that fuelled a U.S. plant. It's rough to see one's market erode in somebody else's direction, but Canada hadn't rushed to erect a tariff wall because, to pick one example from hundreds, U.S. firms enjoyed a seventy-three-percent share of Canadian transportation-equipment sales.

The Americans' position simply didn't hold water. Stumpage assigns a value based on profitable harvest. Conditions vary from province to province (and within a province, too, as you'll realize if you think about southern versus northern B.C.), but generally speaking, bad terrain, worse weather, and greater hauling distances to the nearest mill make harvesting in Canada more difficult than in the U.S. Canadian trees are slower-growing, and accessible forests contain a less valuable mix of logs. All sorts of other variables have to be taken into account, as well, notably the legislated requirement to practise reforestation in Canada. This can be done in several ways. In some cases a forest company pays the provincial government, which then hires people to go out and replant. In others the company itself is responsible, which experience suggests is probably more efficient. Nor can Canadian tax regimes be compared directly with those in place south of the border. Tax laws are an exceedingly arcane subject, but it could well be argued that the capital-gains allowances afforded certain U.S. firms confer a far greater de facto benefit than stumpages ever did.

In order to formulate a real comparison of the two countries' industries, labour rates would have to be factored in. In 1989 B.C. forest workers received on average $28.20 (Can.) an hour. In the Pacific Northwest states, workers struggled by with $17.60 (U.S.). In the American South the average dropped to $14 (U.S.).

In sum the Canadian forest industry is distinct from that of the United States. Similar wood, harvested in similar places and hauled a similar distance, costs more in Canada, and thus a Canadian company makes less per tree. If costs are higher, then stumpage is lower — that's the way our system works. Historically our forest industry has been about half as profitable as the United States'. To be more exact, during the 1980s Canadian forest producers averaged a 3.7-percent return on assets; eight more or less representative American firms earned 4.9 percent. During the same period Canada Savings Bonds returned on average six percent. So much for the widely held perception of the Canadian forest industry as a giant money machine. The fact that Canadian producers achieved success in the U.S. market in the early 1980s hinged on two factors: our dollar was worth about seventy-two cents American, and our mills were demonstrably almost thirty percent more productive than those in the States.

In March 1982 the U.S. Department of Commerce held a series of hearings in Portland, Oregon. Having listened to the American producers' arguments, it found that Canada's stumpage fees were, in some cases, lower, but that this did not entail an unfair subsidy. It did, however, conclude that other Canadian subsidies had contributed to Oregon's loss, but these referred to such things as location grants and modernization programs, which were flying thick and fast as both federal and provincial governments raced each other to establish sawmills and pulp mills wherever fibre was available and development desired. The wisdom of these programs might be debated — and will be, in a later chapter. The point is, the governments involved had every right to go that route if it suited them. It was a domestic matter entirely, just like the use of Municipal Revenue Bonds and infrastructure grants by American states, to which of course Canada did not object.

In any case, the Commerce Department's findings failed to satisfy Senator Packwood and the three firms who'd started the ball rolling — Georgia Pacific, International Paper, and Louisiana Pacific. In October 1982 a group known as the U.S. Coalition for Fair Canadian Lumber Imports — in essence, the original three firms and several more from the southern states — had accumulated a sufficient war chest, and they filed a countervailing-duty petition with the International Trade Commission.

Article 6 of the General Agreement on Tariffs and Trade (GATT) defines a countervailing duty as "a special duty levied for the purpose of offsetting any bounty or subsidy bestowed, directly or indirectly, upon the manufacture, production or export of any merchandise." One can hypothetically catch any number of fish in that sort of net, but the provision had very seldom been invoked — perhaps because it had been originally drafted to address only the most blatant excesses, not to ride herd on the normal activities of governments, which universally seek to attract industries by whatever means they can afford.

Canadian producers were ill-prepared to meet this or any other threat. In 1982 we were represented by something like twenty-five regional trade organizations. Many were little more than a podium for one or two people who could claim, sometimes on flimsy grounds, to represent only local interests. The strongest and by far the best-organized association was British Columbia's Council of Forest Industries (COFI), followed by associations in Quebec and Ontario. Everyone realized at once that there was at least *some* strength in numbers, so I began to contact the major Eastern producers to encourage them to put some money behind a somewhat loose ad hoc coalition of our own — the Eastern Canadian Softwood Lumber Committee. Joined by several smaller producers, we united with COFI, which meant that, because costs were split proportionally based on lumber production, COFI wound up paying about seventy percent of the bills.

COFI's president at this time was Don Lanskail, a husky jolly man who knew the industry inside out. He'd also been a local politician, and eventually served as mayor of North Vancouver. I'm afraid that once or twice his political instincts overrode the logic of a given situation, but he understood better than any of us the pitfalls that lurked in the political arena, as well as the public's sublime lack of interest in complex issues like softwood lumber.

On behalf of COFI Lanskail had already hired a Washington listening post in the person of Herb Fierst, a former trade lawyer well versed in the byzantine manoeuvring that marks the American capital. Fierst suggested that we retain the U.S. law firm of Arnold and Porter to present our defence, and the file was taken over by Robert Herzstein, who was thoroughly familiar with the Department of Commerce, having worked there as an assistant director. We needed all the help we could get, because we weren't getting any support from either the Canadian Embassy in Washington or from the Department of Trade and Commerce in Ottawa.

Meanwhile, to ensure that we could all agree on a course of action, we had the accounting firm of Peat Marwick prepare a data bank that detailed comprehensively — for the first time — the economics of the Canadian forest industry. Various studies had

The author's father and mentor Dr. Hartley Zimmerman pulls a ceremonial switch as chairman of Canada's Defence Research Board.

Duncan Gordon, the author's first boss and leader of both Clarkson Gordon and the Hospital for Sick Children.

Walter Gordon, a model for all citizens as a businessman, public servant, adviser, and philanthropist. *Toronto Star photo*

Gaston Pouliot, one of the greats of
Canada's legal profession and a major
factor in Noranda's Quebec presence.

Another great lawyer, David
Davenport of Vancouver, who guided
Noranda Forest's growth thoroughly
and flawlessly.

The Northwood Board in the early days. Jim McSwiney of Mead, in glasses at left,
answers Alf Powis, second from right, while the rest of us are amused.

First encounter: Knut Grotterod (left), number two at Fraser, with me and John Fisher, later to become head of Fraser, then Southam.

Bud Bird (left), former New Brunswick forestry minister, and Jack Webster, the voice of B.C., handling my daysailer.

Tim Kenny, my partner in Noranda Forest, tries out his loggers equipment gift at his retirement party.

A typical picture of a board. This one, Norcen, was a good one, with members from all over Canada with a common purpose. Chairman Ed Bovey is seated second from left.

A great day as the author's two key business associates, John Bradfield (left) and Alf Powis, welcome him to his company's board of directors.

Takeovers aren't all bad, as this MacMillan Bloedel photo of Ray Smith and Cal Knudsen at an annual general meeting attests. *Vancouver Sun photo*

Monte Hummel of World Wildlife Fund receives Noranda's first $30,000 cheque from its toxicology fund.

The leader, John Turner, stays in shape, settling the world's problems while out on the winter trails.

The ultimate irony: Pat Carney, minister for international trade, presents an export award to Noranda Forest sales president Arkadi Bykhovsky (left) and John Rolland, general manager of Eastern Export Lumber Sales, a year after torpedoing the industry.

Our environmental work was cut out for us, as witness the stacks at Noranda's Horne . . .

. . . and Gaspé smelters.

In the palmy days, common purpose and reasoned debate created good things:
Northwood (above), Noranda Aluminum . . .

. . . Central Canada Potash (above), Hemlo, and Canadian Hunter.

Who knows whether David Suzuki was laughing with me or at me? *Mike Peake, Toronto Sun photo*

Work with the volunteer sector brought Lester Pearson (right) back to the University of Toronto in support of athletics. He is greeted by me (left), U of T chancellor Omand Solandt, and Arnold Wilkinson, warden of Hart House.

previously been done by government advisory committees, but by now they were out of date. This analysis was long overdue and would prove immensely valuable over the long term. It included in-depth records of the industry's production levels, costs and profitability, our financing needs, hauling distances, and countless other factors. We met with the provincial forest ministers, kept our bankers fully apprised of the situation (warning them to brace themselves for an unfavourable resolution), and facilitated a series of meetings that took place in Ottawa between the provincial forest ministers and then U.S. secretary of commerce Malcolm Baldridge.

While all this was going on, the International Trade Commission had made a preliminary ruling in favour of the American producers, the Commerce Department had made a preliminary ruling against them, and the producers had unsuccessfully appealed the latter ruling in the Court of International Trade. Then in May 1983 the Commerce Department issued what's termed a "final negative determination" — unalloyed good news for Canada. It stated that provincial stumpage systems conferred neither an export subsidy nor a countervailable domestic subsidy. In short Canada's position was completely vindicated — at a cost to the Canadian lumber firms of $4-million in legal and consulting fees.

Because there weren't any subsidies, there was no need for a final-injury determination by the International Trade Commission. Nor did the American coalition attempt to seek a further judicial review. Naturally we thought that the case was closed and could be put behind us. In fact, what we'd been through was nothing but the opening skirmish in a war that would begin to rage in earnest in the fall of 1983.

In the wake of the Commerce Department's ruling, American firms began an intensive lobbying campaign that did little more than repeat ad nauseam their now discredited claims. "Subsidized Canadian lumber" was posed as a threat to the American way of life in the forest communities of the Pacific Northwest and the Southeast. It's interesting to note that American consumers, who were being exhorted to support the U.S. producers, were bound to suffer if the American coalition got its way. Stripped of bombast and rhetoric, the U.S. coalition was arguing for higher prices, which would almost certainly result if Canadian firms had to pay a tax or levy or duty of any kind. To recover such a surcharge, we would simply tack it onto our invoices, resulting in more expensive two-by-fours down at the Kansas City lumberyard. The Americans might be sorely tempted to raise their prices to match. The difference would be that we'd have to pay it out, as an operating cost, while they could simply put it into their pockets. The American parents of Canadian subsidiaries were strangely mute on this point throughout the debate. Eventually, though, more than five hundred U.S. building contractors and lumber dealers would unite to form the Coalition to Stop Unfair Wood Tariffs, which basically supported the Canadian position, but seemed to have very little punch.

And so, against all logic, the protectionist bandwagon gathered momentum. The Canadian coalition tried to stay on top of the situation, primarily through our legal firm and Herb Fierst. The federal trade minister, Ed Lumley, turned down our committee's request for a financial contribution to our defence. As usual Ottawa seemed far keener to spend money on trade junkets than to help retain established markets. The government's attitude was that this dispute boiled down to a squabble over stumpage — a provincial issue. As for the provinces, they seemed at times to be silent allies of the Americans. There's no doubt in my mind that many provincial forest ministers had figured out that, if they played their cards right, they could quietly increase their stumpage rates, blame the Americans, and sock the resulting profits into general revenues where stumpage fees had always gone, instead of being more wisely used to support directly enlightened forestry practices. As a result, the provincial forestry departments were chronically starved for funds.

Our coalition's problem was that industry and government were virtual strangers to each other. Contact had been sporadic; there weren't effective lines of communication. The U.S. producers, on the other hand, could sleepwalk their way through the corridors of power. They also had bags of money — donations provided by such industry giants as Georgia Pacific and International Paper.

It soon became obvious that we had to establish an ongoing dialogue with Ottawa and the provinces. Unfortunately this plan ran counter to the Canadian tradition of elite consultation. When politicians finally wake up and decide to take an interest in something, they hasten to form an advisory body that may very well be politically astute, but is scarcely representative of a given industry. Old cronies and unsuccessful former candidates magically rally round; the government tries to create a mix that offends no one and pretends to involve every interested party.

Giving everyone an equal voice doesn't always work, as the coalition soon found out. Don Lanskail, in his position as head of COFI, spoke for the entire B.C. industry, which produced at least two-thirds of the wood; but Tony Rumbold of the Maritime Lumber Bureau was given what amounted to equal time by the media on the grounds that he represented everyone east of Quebec. Maybe he did, but the Maritimes accounted for only about two percent of total Canadian production. This sort of imbalance did not serve our cause well, particularly when the interests of particular regions or groups diverged.

Plainly the forest industry needed what we didn't have: a permanent national association to provide a two-way pipeline between producers and the federal government. Ottawa could retain the option of hearing from or consulting with any individual company or regional body, and it could convene a task force or fact-finding mission if it chose to, but at least there would be an ongoing dialogue to inform public policy. Meanwhile, the association's members would be in constant touch with one another and become more aware of regional concerns. A consensus would probably emerge that, while it wouldn't be perfect, would embrace, reflect, and enhance the interests of all the participants in the Canadian forest industry.

Easier said than done. Getting together twenty-five groups from across our fair and fractious land was a bit like nailing jelly to the wall, but in March 1984 we finally launched the Canadian Forest Industry Council (CFIC). A few small producers opted out, but all the heavyweights came aboard, and eventually we elected as our first president Mike Apsey, who had served as B.C.'s deputy minister of lands and forests before succeeding Lanskail as the head of COFI. As the industry point man, I was named chairman.

THE CFIC'S INITIAL ROLE WAS TO provide a watching brief on trade issues as they directly affected softwood lumber, and to develop measures for use in any subsequent defence of our position. Funding was a perpetual sore point, but we took seriously the warnings of Robert Herzstein, our Washington legal counsel, that the issue could blow up again at any time. We were forced to maintain a state of constant readiness, which meant that there were constant bills to pay. Some members felt that we were going overboard in this regard, but several of those who complained the loudest in fact contributed nothing to the common cause (notably and surprisingly, the Maritimers).

Indeed, the issue moved front and centre during 1985 as the Americans plotted a fresh assault. Antidumping legislation was in the works, and numerous bills were tabled in both Congress and the Senate, all concerned in one way or another with countervailing duties. One was designed to reduce lumber imports to twenty-five percent (and later twenty percent) of the U.S. market. Congress, counting down to an election year, was fired by protectionist enthusiasm, and the U.S. forest industry stepped up its efforts to sway public opinion. The so-called Shamrock Summit in 1985 between Prime Minister Mulroney and President Reagan in Quebec City, at which — after warbling "When Irish Eyes Are Smiling" — they "agreed to give the highest priority to finding mutually acceptable means to reduce and eliminate existing barriers to trade [and to] commit ourselves to halt protectionism in cross-border trade in goods and services" did little or nothing to defuse the dispute.

After an infinity of meetings, consultations, reports, and timber summits, things fired up again in 1986. In May the U.S. Coalition for Fair Lumber Imports petitioned Washington for a twenty-seven percent countervailing duty against Canadian imports. The CFIC's position was to stand and fight, disputing in the proper forum each claim as it arose. We believed that we could once again win the case on its merits. By this time the federal government was displaying a degree of interest, but we were reluctant to pass them the file. The mandarins in Trade and Commerce were far from knowledgeable about the situation, whereas the coalition had been through four years of intensive activity that had by then cost us $7-million. We knew all the players and all the laws; we were prepared, if necessary, to jump through all the hoops all over again, with reasonable confidence of victory.

Part of our strategy was to meet with American legislators who represented key constituencies. At best we could win them over to some degree; at least they'd become better informed. This was deadly serious business, but thanks to Marjorie Kraus, a member of Arnold and Porter's lobbying arm, never boring. Kraus was an entertaining and energetic member of the team, a large woman with an equally expansive view of the world and an even more widespread network of useful contacts. She had honed her skills by running Political Action Committee breakfasts (fundraisers), and seemed thereby to be acquainted with every senator worth his or her salt. Marjorie's style alternated between what I'd call still-fishing and trolling. When practising the former, she would arrange for us to meet a particular legislator, say, George Mitchell of Maine. Mitchell was a strong proponent of the protectionist cause, but when he learned that a Noranda subsidiary operated two sawmills in his home state, he had the grace to listen to us. Kraus's trolling technique involved sauntering through one of the Senate's office buildings, her head swivelling constantly to and fro like a submarine periscope, on the lookout for our targeted prey. If they were in their offices, we would intrude on their time for as long as they would tolerate us.

In the course of these visits I realized for the first time how little even Americans in positions of the highest authority know about Canada. Ninety-nine percent of them probably couldn't have told me where Ontario was. One day I met with Senator John Danforth, vice-chairman of the powerful Banking and Finance Committee, and a staunch protectionist. The only reason I got in to see him was that Noranda owned an aluminum plant in his home state of Missouri. His staff warned me that I'd been allotted fifteen minutes, but that I'd better speak my piece in ten, because Danforth would probably be running late. Surprisingly we spoke for almost an hour. I asked him whether he knew that U.S. trade with Ontario alone was larger than that with Japan, that one-fifth of Canada's GNP consisted of exports of goods and services to the States, that twenty-two percent of America's total exports (more than it shipped to all ten members of the European Economic Community) came in our direction. He didn't, but he was very gracious and said that, while he regretted he'd never been to Canada, no one had bothered to invite him. I promptly did so, and I am still waiting to make good on my invitation.

But pressing flesh and bending senators' ears could take our cause only so far, and I began to think that a concerted effort on the part of the Canadian Embassy in Washington might head off a lot of grief. To this end, I called our newly appointed ambassador, Alan Gotlieb. Gotlieb had been in office only three weeks, had no idea what I was talking about, and probably suspected me of being a crank, but to his credit he at least took the call. I told him that, whether he liked it or not, he was going to hear a lot more about our case — and in that conviction, I was perfectly right.

AT THE BEGINNING OF 1986, CFIC'S defensive efforts were being managed by a new president, Mike Apsey, and seemed to be going well, but suddenly a new element entered the equation. We'd been fixated on our own woes and cares for so long that we'd ignored a whole range of other matters — the East Coast fisheries, the remains of the ill-fated national energy program, and so on down the list. From Ottawa's point of view, softwood lumber was just another burr under the saddle when it came to settling a much larger package of cross-border issues that were lumped together under the heading of free trade, a concept that was almost totally unfamiliar to the forest industry.

In 1984 Mulroney's Conservatives had campaigned on the basis that free trade didn't much interest them. Instead, they proposed to enhance "fair" trade by concentrating on specific sectors, as had been done with the Auto Pact, textile manufacturing, pulp and paper, and metals such as zinc and copper. This policy was fine with the forest industries; we'd always sold our products at world prices. Our contacts spanned the globe and, although there was always room for improvement, we were selling everything we made. We were certainly already making real inroads into the American market — hence that market's panic reaction.

In retrospect it's clear that after the Shamrock Summit the free-trade initiative became Job One in Ottawa. Few Canadians grasped the federal government's almost desperate urgency to fast-track the negotiations. The Tories wanted a clean slate, and the most conspicuous and contentious blot on that slate was the dispute over softwood lumber, the largest protectionist action in Canada–U.S. history. The industry was suddenly reduced to little more than a bargaining chip in the much larger free-trade negotiations. The Americans were confident that they could easily rid the negotiations of this pesky issue. In April 1986 Clayton Yeutter, the U.S. chief negotiator, had assured David Pryor, the Democratic Senator from Arkansas — in words that conjured up neutering a bothersome household pet — "we'll get lumber fixed."

This intention was obviously shared by President Reagan, who on May 5 wrote to Senator Packwood that he intended to seek an "expedited resolution . . . independent of the comprehensive negotiations. If this cannot be achieved through bilateral negotiations with Canada, then I will take such action as may be necessary to resolve this problem consistent with U.S. law." On May 23 he imposed a thirty-five-percent tariff on shakes and shingles. Mulroney responded by calling the action "unjustifiable" and "appalling." Canada announced its intention to retaliate. The Department of Commerce weighed in with yet another countervailing duty investigation. Ambassador Gotlieb, a shrewd but biased observer of American politics, remarked that even if the countervailing duty case was won, "new legislation could be passed by Congress." However, he urged that the case be fought, a view supported by Joe Clark, Canada's external affairs minister.

In June things in Ottawa went from bad to worse when Jim Kelleher, the federal minister of international trade, a reasonable and experienced former business lawyer who'd been helpful to us, was replaced by novice minister Pat Carney, whose appointment at this critical juncture was mystifying to many observers. One theory had it that Mulroney put Carney in place to ensure that the wheels would come off the softwood dispute, helping to clear the decks for the free-trade negotiations. Like many rookie ministers, Carney tried to hit a home run the first time she stepped up to the plate.

Another new personality entered the picture when Bill Vander Zalm was sworn in as premier of British Columbia. Vander Zalm had always struck me as a flake, with no clearly defined philosophy or grip on the issues, but his buffoonish manner was deceptive. Toward the end of his tenure in office, years after the softwood dispute, I took him to lunch in Toronto. During our conversation it became clear he had known far more than he'd let on at the time; he had understood the issues exactly and had played dumb for his own good purposes. The same, however, could not be said for the man he appointed as his new forestry minister. In private life Jack Kempf had been a logging contractor in northern B.C. who'd lost his contract with Buckley Valley because the company wasn't satisfied with his performance. On assuming his portfolio, he was quick to announce an immediate review of provincial forest policies, adding that, in his opinion, stumpage rates were too low, and that he'd suspected for many years that the province hadn't been getting a good return from the industry.

In July 1986 the CFIC convened in Vancouver to debate the options. Many members felt that we'd have to saw off, and the idea of a temporary and fully refundable export tax was discussed in some detail. This proposal had its drawbacks — notably, that the industry could ill afford it — but it would at least serve as an interim solution, quieting all the claimants down until the issue could be finally, fairly, and objectively adjudicated. If, as we were convinced, the Canadian position eventually won the day, the monies would stay in Canada and could be paid back to the industry in time.

This proposition was put to Carney in late July. We outlined our case in detail and tried to bring her up to speed on the complexities of the issue. After a couple of intensive meetings, during which she pledged to act as an "honest broker" for the provinces, we agreed to support her in future negotiations with the Americans — but only if she held to her promise that the absolute furthest she would go was a five-percent export tax. She displayed little enthusiasm for this idea.

The next week the CFIC learned that four provinces — B.C., Alberta, Ontario, and Quebec — had put together a scheme, independent of Ottawa, to increase stumpage fees by something like $370-million (which equalled what would have been raised by a *ten*-percent export tax). Emboldened by this development, the American coalition immediately raised the ante and petitioned for a countervailing duty of thirty-three to thirty-six percent.

On September 30 Carney put the stumpage-hike proposal to Malcolm Baldridge, the American secretary of commerce. She termed it a once-only, take-it-or-leave-it offer. Baldridge left it, and the Americans labelled Carney "good old once-only Pat."

This was a particularly unfortunate period for the CFIC. Carney's meanderings were bad enough, but the coalition, for its part, failed to present a united front when it came to stepping up our political activity in Washington. John Kerr, a member of the CFIC executive and the president of Lignum Incorporated, had suggested that we employ yet another Washington lobbyist, a legal firm including Walter Mondale, the former Democratic presidential candidate. We met with Mondale and his partner, John Riley, a Runyonesque character who always wore bright yellow braces and no jacket. His claim to fame was that he'd managed Mondale's campaign, which was not an altogether sterling recommendation. Kerr wanted to strike a deal at once — literally, that very afternoon — because he was in a rush to catch a plane.

After he left the meeting, I told Mondale and Riley that, as the CFIC's chairman and keeper of the purse, I'd have to consult with the membership. Kerr was embarrassed by this and became unforgivably annoyed with me. This incident was the only serious rift in our campaign. I admired Kerr in many ways, but he took a permanent scunner to me. Today he has the satisfaction of being CFIC's 1996 chairman and negotiator of the latest deal on the matter. Through all of this Mike Apsey has remained the nursemaid, father confessor, and voice or reason.

On October 16, even though reports from three different consulting firms had identified major flaws in the Americans' countervailing-duty petitions, the Department of Commerce turned around and contradicted its earlier finding, weighing in with yet another preliminary determination. This one approved the idea of a fifteen-percent preliminary duty to take effect at year end, a scenario described by Carney as "deplorable, artificial, and contrived." It was certainly expensive. Fifteen percent of total imports amounted to $500-million: in other words, more than the profits of the entire industry. (Later, this figure would bounce around. When Mulroney mentioned $700-million, he was talking about the same calculation. The total varies because the volume and worth of softwood shipments fluctuate.) Our only hope was that the Commerce Department's ruling was contingent upon further examination by the International Trade Commission, which would have to determine that subsidies existed and then arrive at the extent of damages caused. Of course, we felt that subsidies didn't exist, and we geared up to present our case all over again.

But matters were already being taken out of our hands. The silence from Ottawa was deafening. On October 24 I wrote to Mulroney asking for a face-to-face meeting. Unfortunately his schedule did not permit a response until three weeks had passed. The guy who barred the door, Bernard Roy, Mulroney's chief of staff, later became a director of Noranda — an ironic appointment for someone I viewed as a one-dimensional political operator who had acted against our interests.

Nor could coalition members fathom the apparent actions of Ambassador Gotlieb, who seemed determined to ingratiate himself with the Americans at any cost. This was either his mandate or his ambition; I never figured out which or in what proportion. Depending on which scenario you credit, he either convinced or was instructed by Ottawa that the Canadian forest industry faced a losing battle.

The manoeuvrings continued unabated. During one meeting, a briefing session at a Toronto hotel, I got my dander up and lectured a collection of forestry ministers to the effect that "you people have got to understand you work for *us*. You don't work for you. *Our* interest is the public interest. You are public servants and you have to damn well understand our situation."

But how could they? In one sense they didn't know what it was. I looked around the gathering and suddenly realized I was one of only two people in the room who'd been with the issue since the beginning. All the other faces — premiers, ministers and deputy ministers, mandarins, and hangers-on — had changed.

I wrote to Pat Carney, copying five premiers whose provinces were most affected by the softwood issue. I stressed that, to my mind, the best course remained a vigorous fight on all fronts, but that if the International Trade Commission determined that subsidies in fact existed, "presumably Canada can express its enormous disappointment and, at the same time, propose an immediate replacement of U.S. countervailing-duty collections with a Canadian export tax, so at least to keep the revenues in Canada." By this I meant a tax in the range of five percent, which Carney very well knew.

On October 21 the federal and provincial governments met with industry executives and pledged to fight on rather than negotiate on the basis of the Commerce Department's latest fifteen-percent duty ruling. But within weeks this more-or-less united front developed cracks. On November 18 the first ministers' conference kicked off in Ottawa with the usual round of motherhood statements before reconvening in Vancouver two days later to focus on trade. On November 19 Jack Kempf announced that B.C. had sought legal advice with a view to cutting its own deal with the States. That very day, with no warning to the industry, Carney offered Baldridge a settlement based on a fifteen-percent export tax, in return for which the U.S. would withdraw its countervailing-duty petition.

In Vancouver the premiers were urged to get behind this proposal, so as to get the free-trade negotiations under way. Many premiers liked the looks of a tax (never mind how high) that would be collected by customs at the border, then funnelled into their general revenues. The alternative, a duty collected and retained by the Americans, was unattractive.

I was at a dinner party in Toronto when a call came through from Simon Reisman, Canada's chief negotiator, who was closeted in the Vancouver meeting. He asked me to bring the industry on-side. (Some reports suggested that he asked me to "shut up" about the softwood issue. He didn't, but Michael Wilson, the Minister of Finance, did at a later date, when he became minister of international trade.) I told

Reisman that I had no authority to commit the industry to anything without consultation, that I knew already what our answer would be, and that I disagreed violently with what Carney was doing. To no avail. Nine premiers supported the federal proposal. Ontario's David Peterson had conferred with me before flying to Vancouver (he'd invited me to accompany him) and explained that Canadian unity was paramount in his mind and he wouldn't vote against whatever consensus might emerge. I respected that view and wasn't surprised when he abstained from the vote.

The federal government quickly began to beat its own drum. Mulroney told Knowlton Nash on CBC television's "The National" that the tax was "going to make some people unhappy, but it's the right thing to do. You know, you go ahead and say, 'Fight, fight, fight!' You lose, and you've got $700-million sitting in someone else's pocket — not in B.C.'s or Quebec's or Ontario's. So be it. We've done it. We will take the consequences from the private sector or armchair critics, whoever they are. As prime minister, I'm not going to sit on Adam Zimmerman's front porch while the economy of British Columbia is being jeopardized." Another CBC reporter, Karen Webb, asked me whether the fight was too important to be left to the politicians. I replied that I'd want my heart bypass done by the most skilled cardiac surgeon, not the president of the hospital.

In early December, having informed the House that I'd asked her to negotiate on the industry's behalf (a statement that implied a nonexistent carte blanche and thus was totally misleading), Carney went vacationing in Hawaii, while her staff burned the midnight oil in Washington. With the clock running, on December 30 Canada and the U.S. signed a Memorandum of Understanding, ensuring that Canada would introduce an export-charge act to levy the fifteen-percent tax, which could, however, be offset by whatever increases in stumpages were invoked by the provinces. In the event, all the provinces raised their stumpages an appropriate amount and so got the money, anyway. In return, the Department of Commerce terminated its investigation. Disgracefully all these activities were subject to review and approval by the Americans, who would "monitor closely the operation of the agreement" to make sure that sums collected by either the export charge or any subsequent measures "are not returned to, or otherwise used to benefit" the lumber industry. The federal government thus allowed our foreign competitors to dictate how much we ought to pay for our own timber. So much for what little remains of Canadian economic sovereignty.

So there we were, cast adrift by Ottawa, at odds with the provinces, facing the prospect of a fifteen-percent tax for the foreseeable future, and out of pocket more than $10-million in legal and consulting fees (the meter kept running there, too). It soon became apparent that, as we'd feared, the provincial regimes seized upon increased stumpages as an excuse to pad their coffers. (In 1987 Jack Kempf announced that none of B.C.'s stumpage hikes — an estimated $350-million in total — would be put toward reforestation programs. This prompted Carney to remark in the House that B.C.'s forests were a "silvicultural slum." The next day Vander Zalm contradicted Kempf and would later relieve him of his no doubt onerous duties.) But in the end some good has come of this. The provinces ultimately agreed that stumpage fees would be channelled directly to the departments of forestry, which has led to a number of measurable improvements in the forests in intervening years.

On December 30, the day the Memorandum of Understanding was signed, Carney took a moment to send me a reproving letter. In it she said that I had "fail[ed] to see what we have achieved by the agreement. You have clearly misinterpreted our success in preserving Canadian sovereignty. Finally, perhaps you don't care about keeping the funds from the export charge in Canada. To you, perhaps it's merely a cost of doing business, and you don't care if the money is siphoned off to the U.S." And so on. This letter was simultaneously released to the media and sent to me by courier. It being New Year's, I finally got it on January 2 or 3. Its progress was slowed by the fact that it came attached to a large and imposing menorah, the cande-labrum lit during Hanukkah.

This gesture was hard to fathom, but, charitable as always, I thought that Carney might have assumed I was Jewish and wanted to make a sort of peace offering. Not so. Actually one of her staff had taped the letter to the menorah, which stood in the lobby of the External Affairs building. The courier, assuming that message and menorah were all of a piece, delivered both to me. This scenario dawned on me only when frantic phone calls started to arrive from External Affairs. I thanked the callers for their wonderful gift and said it would have an honoured place in my office. This resulted in even more frantic appeals for its return. I sent the menorah back to them eventually, but not before I had a picture taken that shows me standing beside it. Carney, when she heard of this, was not amused.

The Free Trade Agreement was finally signed on October 4, 1987. It included a vital dispute-settlement provision, which seemed to offer a measure of hope and struck me at the time as the most important element of an otherwise imperfect accord. But no provision is iron-clad, and this one appears to have failed us in 1996 as the Americans resurrect their protectionist agenda.

The bottom line was that the Canadian lumber industry was forced to shell out an extra fifteen percent in the form of increased stumpage fees. We received not one penny's support from the federal government to defray our campaign's legal or other costs. Instead, Ottawa spent an estimated $13-million to promote the FTA. Noranda Inc., as a member of the Canadian Alliance for Trade and Job Opportunities, contributed $200,000 toward a $5-million pro-FTA campaign. MacMillan Bloedel, which we controlled at the time, got touched for a portion of this amount. Remarkably, as chair-man of Noranda Forest, I was not canvassed!

The absence of an approach to the head of Noranda Forest may have reflected the fact that it was a big, albeit huge, subsidiary company, but it may also have reflected the perception that the chairman of the company (me) was not on the free trade side. Perhaps stupidly, I was unaware of any huge momentum building in the public for free trade, although I did know there were a few well-known apostles for whom there was something in it. As a long-time resource executive, I believed we were already largely in a free-trade environment and were able to compete; our real need was for a dispute-settlement mechanism.

I thought that John Turner did a masterful job in arguing the "nay" side, but then Turner always was a cut above many of his critics in his understanding of the matter. He knew that Canadians would pay the ultimate sacrifice for free trade — their sovereignty. He knew that the Americans would continue to play protectionism, as they have, and he knew that no proposed deal had been objectively analysed.

Turner had an election to fight on the issue which he might have won, had not big business united against him. Certainly I would not have fought him, as he is my friend. For my part, I had the responsibility of understanding what the deal meant to my business. Although I shared many of Turner's perceptions, in the end the prospect of a workable dispute-settlement mechanism won my vote.

I believe now, more strongly than ever, that the deal we got was not very good as we see it being abrogated or run aground regularly by the Americans. Witness softwood lumber. We might have made good sectoral deals had the issues been better researched and analysed, and we would not have been so overwhelmed by everything American as we are today. Ask the movie-makers, booksellers, mass-merchandisers, furniture makers, and parts manufacturers.

———•••———

BY 1991 CANADA WAS MIRED IN yet another recession. Our share of the U.S. softwood-lumber market had dropped from thirty-three to twenty-six percent, its lowest level in thirteen years. British Columbia, which (along with Alberta and Quebec) had raised its stumpage rates, now complained loud and long that the Memorandum of Understanding with the Americans had cost the province seven thousand jobs. Claude Richmond, the province's newly appointed forestry minister (it's a revolving door out there) blamed "stumpage rates that aren't sensitive to the market . . . I've been very offended by an agreement that ties our hands." Mr. Richmond was not alone in this regard.

In September 1991 Prime Minister Mulroney met with President Reagan's successor, George Bush, in Maine, and served notice that Ottawa would cancel the Memorandum of Understanding on October 4. Washington didn't even bother with ritual sabre-rattling. It ruled that Canadian exporters had to post a fifteen-percent bond instead of a lumber duty on all shipments to the U.S. The Department of Commerce self-initiated yet another countervailing-duty case without waiting for a petition from American industry. Mike Wilson, Canada's newly appointed minister of international trade, said that Canada would appeal to GATT. Thus, he said, the government would "support the Canadian lumber industry and combat the Americans." Seized by sudden bellicosity, Mulroney chimed in with the vow that "we're going to fight this action very vigorously."

Canada lost the first round hands down. On December 16 the International Trade Commission voted three to nothing to press the case that softwood imports were hurting American industry. By March 5, 1992, the Department of Commerce had accepted the age-old argument that low Canadian stumpage (which by then had been raised sky-high) equalled subsidy. A new charge surfaced, as well: Canada's ban on exporting raw logs to U.S. mills allowed Canadian mills to buy timber for less than they would pay in an open, cross-border market. The department promptly slapped a preliminary duty of 14.48 percent on all Canadian lumber. A senior official was quoted as saying, "The only remaining question is, how large the final permanent duty will be." The answer, which surfaced on May 28, was 6.5 percent — on the theory that Canadian softwood exports (which as I've said, had dropped appreciably) were placing at risk 16,000

American jobs. Canada promptly appealed this finding to the dispute-settlement panel.

As 1992 wound on, Canada began to feel the negative impact of the Free Trade Agreement as a whole. Capital migrated southward. U.S.-dominated pharmaceutical firms were granted a virtual monopoly position in the Canadian market, so that Canadian consumers could no longer purchase cheaper generic drugs. In a deal kept under wraps until its announcement could have little effect on his chances for reelection, Mulroney juggled our banking regulations, allowing American Express unprecedented access to the Canadian financial market. Even salmon went down for the count when Peter Murphy, the U.S. trade negotiator, pressured Mulroney into scrapping a 1908 law that demanded B.C. salmon had to be processed before export. Now the blameless fish were trucked south to American plants.

And lo and behold, even Canada's original negotiators had begun to entertain second thoughts. Gordon Ritchie, once a senior member of the FTA team, declared that "American authorities have been protecting special interests through an array of aggressive actions . . . getting dangerously close to systematic abuse of the letter and spirit of the agreement." Simon Reisman was even more explicit: "The Americans are bastards. They're behaving like thugs, taking every advantage they can, and coming close to crossing the line." Well, what did Ritchie and Reisman expect? They'd sat across the table from these guys for months on end. If that didn't give them a realistic insight into who they were facing, perhaps they should have investigated some other line of work.

In mid-December 1993 the five-member binational dispute panel released its findings, which criticized the Commerce Department for "totally ignoring evidence, advancing illogical arguments, and messing up the arithmetic." In a three-to-two decision it ruled that the Americans had failed to provide a rational basis for the 6.5-percent provisional duty.

In March 1994 the ITC voted to challenge the panel on the

grounds that two of the three Canadian representatives had failed to disclose a possible conflict of interest, in that they were members of legal firms that, in the past, had acted for Canadian lumber companies (as if you could find a firm that had not!). But on August 4 of that year a rarely convened extraordinary-challenge committee upheld the dispute-settling panel's decision. More than $800-million in border taxes, bonds, and duties would have to be refunded, along with appropriate interest, to Canadian exporters. And the ten-year dispute (or so we thought) was over.

But not so fast! You may remember a series of horror films from the 1950s, in which the monster, mutant, or amorphous blob is zapped with bursts of electricity and fired back into outer space. The words "The End" appeared on the screen, followed by the provocative postscript "Or Is It?"

In February 1996 Canadians learned that softwood had come back to haunt them. Very briefly, a deal (or, rather, a series of deals) was struck that — according to Art Eggleton, the newly anointed federal minister of trade — would result in "five years of peace." If the arrangements are ratified, B.C. will "voluntarily" impose quotas on shipments to the States. If the quotas are exceeded, Ottawa will step in and levy a two-tiered export tax, rendering the shipments unprofitable. Quebec, Alberta, and Ontario, on the other hand, will hike their stumpage fees. Combined, these measures will serve to decrease Canada's export volumes by at least ten percent. In return, the Americans have pledged not to launch any further countervailing actions until the year 2001.

These arrangements were negotiated somewhat independently by the provinces themselves, then brought together under the aegis of the federal government. It would appear that the deal, rather than assuring half a decade's peace and quiet, will set a dangerous precedent of allowing the provinces to pursue individual courses of action when it comes to international trade; result in an administrative nightmare (it's difficult to track the province of origin of a given shipment, because softwood moves around Canada before it's shipped abroad); line the pockets of the provincial regimes while possibly rendering some of their industries uncompetitive (Quebec's stumpage rates, for example, have doubled); and fail to appease the U.S. in any event. Actually, in the end the deal became simply a quota deal for all provinces, administered from Ottawa. Having made the obligatory mention of a level playing field, Mickey Kantor, the current American trade representative, was quoted as stating that, if the deal didn't work out to his satisfaction, he would consider it void and pursue other measures. (As this book was being prepared for publication, the aforementioned John Kerr, president of Lignum, had a letter published in the *Financial Post* praising the latest lumber deal, noting that he negotiated it. God bless him if it really works.)

Why didn't Canada continue to place its faith in the binational dispute-settlement mechanism? Because in the interim U.S. law has changed. The dispute panel, which still exists, is limited in its powers and can only determine whether or not trade bodies interpret laws (on either side of the border) correctly. Hence, Eggleton's haste to cut a deal of some description, and Kerr's admission that, if the panel were resorted to, "it would be harder [for Canada] to win another case." This led *Globe and Mail* columnist Terence Corcoran to remark that the dominoes have started to go down. He noted that certain tariffs levied by Canada on American farm products have been challenged by the U.S., and that the dispute is currently before yet another settlement panel. But, according to Corcoran, "in the end, it probably won't matter who wins . . . by caving in to the United States on softwood lumber, Mr. Eggleton has endorsed the idea that the panel process has no force."

I would agree, and I view with mounting dismay a great many of Canada's dealings with our neighbours to the south. I can't in all honesty say that the Free Trade Agreement has had a universally negative impact. It came at precisely the wrong time, and its negative effect was exacerbated by high interest rates, high taxes, a difficult labour situation, and an adverse currency exchange. It was imposed (never the best way to proceed) by a federal government that had changed its tune and committed itself to a sweeping new economic agenda. Mulroney, aided by the Business Council on National Issues, found enough allies to carry the day. He wanted friends and supporters in the business world on both sides of the border, but friends are expensive to buy. Some of Mulroney's allies have been repaid in the usual ways. Some sit beside Pat Carney in the Senate, while others count their corporate and personal blessings.

A full discussion of what free trade has meant for Canada has already filled several books and will fill several more. I suspect that in many cases it hasn't meant all that much, other than exposing Canadian industries to competition on a different scale. But most businesses had already competed in the States and elsewhere with some measure of success. The Americans are no smarter than we are. They don't do any better than we do, given the famous level playing field; it's just that a market twelve times our size does much to convey that erroneous impression. I lament the fact that various Canadian businesses are held hostage to that market in a pervasive and destructive way, and I maintain that free trade has done absolutely nothing one way or the other for our national identity and culture. We had already become more Americanized, and that one-way osmosis will continue to take place across the world's longest undefended border.

Certainly the forest industry learned valuable lessons from the defence that we mounted during the 1980s and early 1990s. To a degree we were the authors of our own misfortune. The CFIC came together in response to a clearly defined crisis, but eventually fragmented and disengaged from the fight. Its demise illustrates both the natural human inability to preserve a consensus, and the stupidity of trying to fight a battle in isolation, but these lessons seem to have gone unlearned.

If free trade were being negotiated today, would the deal be signed with such alacrity? I believe so. The argument that Canada must of necessity be aligned with a trading block would win out. Would the forest industry still be thrown to the wolves? Reflect on the events I've just described and decide for yourself. I suppose that at least the industry — and all Canadians — have learned the hard way that the Americans play hardball. And that the fat lady hasn't even begun to sing her final aria.

6

Always the Environment

In the 1930s when my family lived in Niagara Falls, New York, there was no such thing as an environmental movement. Every day we were subjected to an array of noxious emissions from the city's thriving electrochemical industries. I learned early on what it was like to be on the receiving end of pollution, and it's absolutely astonishing to think back on the conditions that prevailed right up the street from our house. Enormous plants — Carborundum, Hooker Chemical, Matheson Alkali, and Union Carbide — were spewing forth a filthy cloud of God only knew what. Chlorine was the principal element in the mix, which did wonders for our nasal passages. Fresh air was a relative term, and even when you were inside a car you sometimes wanted to hold your breath; otherwise lungs would feel seared and eyes would start to water. The tap water was so foul-tasting that my mother used to buy our supplies by the bottle.

But people shrugged these environmental shortcomings off as a fact of life — the price you paid for having a job when jobs were few and far between. The electrochemical plants were the building blocks of the city's economy, and nobody was about to tinker with success. Even if someone had wanted to attack the problem, it's hard to imagine where they'd have begun, because the technology wasn't available to bring about a cure. So the green cloud was left to drift away, out of sight and mind, and whatever was in the water (the solution to pollution was dilution) went rushing over Niagara Falls.

Not much had improved by the time I got my first summer job at the Marathon Pulp Mill on the north shore of Lake Superior. Although the mill was brand-new, there was no treatment for the liquid effluent that was pumped directly into Lake Superior, and the gases emitted by the mill's smokestacks smelled like rotten eggs, as did the emissions from every other kraft-process pulp mill in the world. The villains were chemical compounds known as mercaptans, which are loaded with sulphur. Thanks to scrubbers, retrofits, and other processes, today's mills have gone a long way toward eliminating the stench. Back in the 1940s, however, there was no escaping it, but this did not faze the townsfolk who joked about "the smell of money."

Nor had environmental perfection been reached by the late 1950s, which is when I arrived at the Rouyn-Noranda plant, whose two towering stacks dispersed the gases from the copper-smelting process. One day I happened to be out on the local golf course with the plant manager when we were suddenly enveloped by a cloud of sulphur dioxide. I was depressed to be told that this was a "typical inversion." In other words, what was supposed to go up had come down with a vengeance. My lungs were much the worse for wear, and the grass where we stood was actually yellowed.

These and many other experiences combined to put me on the side of environmental change when I was in a position to effect it —

and when technology enabled industry to respond. Not the least influence was my family, all of whom were trained and knowledgeable about "environmentalism." Also, I was always disposed to make an effort to see the other person's point of view, to examine seriously the validity of divergent beliefs, and to get my own in order before I acted on them or jumped to conclusions. I'm not and have never been an apostle of unbridled development at any cost. There's no doubt that the cumulative impact of decades of industrialization has had a damaging impact on the environment. No sensible person could argue otherwise, but what troubles me is the one-sided allocation of blame. It's easy to target big industry; any form of industrial activity inevitably inflicts some damage on the natural surroundings. So does building a subdivision in what was once a farmer's field. The question is, is the damage tolerable or not? My assertion is that industry overall — in particular the Canadian forest industry — behaves far more responsibly than those who attempt to place it in the pillory.

The realization that times had changed began to dawn on me in the mid-1970s, and I can recall a couple of defining moments with utmost clarity.

The first came in my capacity as executive vice-president when I addressed an annual meeting of Noranda. Directly in front of me were a group of student environmental activists from Queen's University — well dressed and well educated, the sort of young people corporate recruiters fall over themselves to hire. I looked up from my notes to see one of them mouth the word "motherfucker."

The second came in the winter of 1976, at a time when my daughter Barbara was heading toward a career in environmental affairs. Noranda had recently taken over the Fraser Companies' Edmundston, New Brunswick, pulp mill, an aging facility that cried out for modernization. She and a friend named Kathy Goldsmith were hired to help establish baselines of the environmental degradation at hand — a fancy way of saying, to figure out how much damage had already been done, and what measures were necessary to remedy it. One of her first letters home ran as follows: "Just so you know, Dad, this place isn't pollution, it's gross pollution, and it really needs quick fixing."

That assessment was totally valid, and we were in fact already fixing it as fast as we could. But I should add that Barbara's criticism was not totally unexpected. Many an evening at the family dinner table, I sat with a thoroughly informed and highly argumentative group of four Zimmerman children, aided and abetted by my wife, who told me in no uncertain terms that they were less than proud of what I and my company were doing.

In the 1950s, when my career began, business was less beset. Provided that a firm operated according to the licences, permits, and laws of the jurisdiction concerned, nobody gave it any hassle. The priority in Canada — indeed, in every developed and developing country in the world — was to exploit more and more resources of every kind in response to a burgeoning population and ever increasing public demand for industrial products.

Industry was not completely irresponsible. Every new plant had to and did employ the latest pollution-control technology. Tailings ponds were left untouched, but we learned how to grass them over. Pulp-mill effluent wasn't always treated, but at least it was thinned out, so as not to harm fish even in the immediate vicinity. Forestry practices were rather more careless and far more wasteful. Loggers left behind massive quantities of debris and neglected such problems as stream-bank erosion and landslides that stemmed from logging-road construction. Reforestation took place, but not nearly as diligently as it should have. The concept of sustainable yield was more honoured in the breach than in the observance. This was the frontier mentality at work. Canada had endless acres of trees; if you ran out, you could always go farther north and find some more. There were miles and miles of rivers; they would wash our sins away. Mill workers may have had a hard time breathing, but on a broader scale, getting the ore out of the ground or the trees off the mountainside overrode any concern about the environment.

People needed and wanted what was emerging from the mines and the mills. Consumers drove the agenda. If industry had said, "You're going to have to pay more for paper towels so that the mill towns will smell nicer," we'd have met with a frosty reception. In retrospect, the environmental measures we took may seem primitive, just as the ones we practise today may be deemed insufficient half a century from now, but they were all we had to work with at the time.

Prior to the 1970s environmental problems had largely been thrashed out between the industrial producers and federal, provincial, or state lawmakers. But when the decade began, a spate of third parties, the special- or single-interest groups, chief among them World Wildlife, the Sierra Club, and Greenpeace, were spawning thick and fast. At first their efforts were more or less localized. But not for long, because they soon learned how to present their cases to the media in dramatic and emotionally charged ways. At worst, some of these appeals were ill-founded on fiction or frankly malicious. They cited questionable studies, exaggerated the real or imagined dangers, and made unreasonable, often flat-out impossible demands. These were presented to a sometimes credulous public that hadn't heard industry's side of things, because we'd never had to articulate it.

Initially I thought that anything that served to focus attention on the environment and brought a broader public voice into the debate over how large-scale resource industries should be operated was long overdue, almost certainly inevitable, and potentially a step forward. I knew that the environmental lobby would make life more difficult for Noranda, but I acknowledged that the lobby represented progress of a kind.

Acid rain was the first environmental hurdle that Noranda had to overcome. I well remember opening up a report that named the company as the second-largest point source of sulphur-dioxide emissions in North America. This referred to our twin stacks at

Rouyn-Noranda, the ones that had sent me reeling on the golf course. Plainly we bore some degree of responsibility here, but the issue wasn't black and white. We could cry mea culpa and shut down, in which case somebody else would have taken the plant over and opened it up again, or we could work toward a solution. But because the problem wasn't entirely of our own making, we were unwilling to shoulder more than our fair share of the burden when it came to a cure. Provided the competition had to adopt the same measures — which they did — we were willing to sit down with the regulatory agencies involved so as to arrive at a series of achievable goals and a sensibly paced remedial process, bounded by the limits of technical capability and ever present financial constraints.

Acid rain is a handy euphemism for the lowering of the pH levels in precipitation as a result of the combination of sulphur-dioxide and nitrous-dioxide emissions in the upper atmosphere. Its effects were first observed in Ontario's cottage country, notably the Muskoka lakes. Their waters looked pretty enough, having been clarified to a brilliant blue-green, but the fish were dead and dying. As the rock had no limestone, there was no possibility of neutralizing the acidity.

At first glance the culprits were easy enough to identify. The prime offenders were thought to be Rouyn-Noranda's twin stacks, Inco's superstack at Copper Cliff, outside Sudbury, and Ontario Hydro's Lakeview power plant in Toronto's west end. Lesser, though still likely, sources were the Hudson Bay smelter at Flin Flon, Manitoba, the Algoma steel plant in Sault Ste. Marie, and the Dofasco and Stelco furnaces in Hamilton. All these were convenient targets because of their imposing size, and few bothered to look farther afield, to the Ohio Valley and the coal-fired power plants of the American Midwest.

Those who tried to investigate other causes did not fare very well. Noranda monitored sixty lakes within a five-hundred-kilometre radius downwind of the twin stacks and found little evidence of acidic conditions. When Inco shut down its operations for a nine-month period, there was no measurable change in pH readings. It was suggested that certain lakes were simply overfished; that maple trees, rather than suffering acid-rain-related dieback, were simply getting old. To no avail. Industry was branded the sole offender, and everyone else got off scot-free — including several million motorists. These were the days before catalytic converters and unleaded gasoline. North America's cars, trucks, and other vehicles produced vastly more sulphur dioxide and nitrous dioxide than all its smelters and thermal-electrical-generating plants combined. Automobile-pollution-control technology has improved, but ill-tuned cars continue to play their part; witness, for example, car-crazy Los Angeles, which, although not awash in heavy industry, is cloaked in smog.

Noranda was willing to do its part to reduce emissions by moving away from "reverbatory furnace" smelting to a continuous smelting process. This produced quantities of pure sulphur dioxide, which could then be recaptured and turned into sulphuric acid. The modifications cost a great deal of money (Noranda spent upwards of $75-million), but the acid could then, theoretically, be sold on the commercial market.

At about the same time, Noranda decided to seize the initiative by establishing an office of environmental affairs. We were lucky to have on staff a remarkable man named Frank Frantisak, who became one of the most significant participants in industry's attempts to deal with environmental issues.

Frantisak had emigrated from Czechoslovakia, having spent the Second World War fighting with the underground and hiding from the Nazis, so he was ready for anything when he got to Canada. He worked first for the Ontario government, then for Inco as a senior environmental engineer. Inco was one of the first companies to wrestle with environmental woes because of its difficulties in and around Sudbury. Its early processes had involved so-called direct-smelting ores, which were simply laid out on the ground and burned to get rid of waste elements, particularly sulphur. This expedient killed every growing thing for miles around and resulted in a stark and barren moonscape. Inco had its environmental work cut out — but so did Noranda.

Frantisak grew disenchanted with the Inco job, went to work with a firm of consulting engineers, then worked with the provincial government again, before he was brought to Noranda by Alex Balogh, the senior head of metallurgy. When I became president, Frank was the logical and by far the best choice for the brand-new and at the time unique position of director of environmental affairs.

It's fair to say that, thanks to his practical experience, Frank was well ahead of many environmentalists when it came to identifying problems and posing workable solutions. He was courteous and disciplined, knew exactly what he was talking about, and eventually became renowned in both the mining and forest-products industries.

In 1983 Frank, Alex Balogh, and I embarked on what amounted to a cross-Canada tour of the editorial boards of major newspapers. The primary focus was acid rain. Because we'd done our homework, we could state with a fair degree of certainty what Noranda's plants were emitting, where the emission ended up, and what could be done to cut back on it at the source. We also met with individual print and broadcast journalists. This wasn't a public-relations dog-and-pony show. We believed that we knew the subject as well or better than anybody, and that by presenting straightforward explanations we could enhance future coverage of the debate. We certainly got far more press attention than we'd anticipated, but it's difficult to judge how well we succeeded in our aims. Looking back, I think that the rigid battle lines hadn't yet been drawn. The media (who weren't themselves acquainted with the facts) were more inclined to give us a fair hearing; they treated our meetings as briefing sessions, a chance to digest complex and highly technical information. We were the first to admit that we didn't have all the answers, but we weren't trying to hide anything. For a time we managed to make the debate more open to reasoned and reasonable conclusions.

Thanks to Frank, our position was always clear; we could validate what we were saying and were seen to be acting forthrightly and responsibly, having at least given environmental matters serious consideration. A critic might fault our means of addressing them, but it was undeniable that we'd thought them through. It's folly to mount a superficial public-relations effort if you haven't got your facts straight.

Frank made sure that Noranda was present and accounted for at the World Industrial Conference on Environmental Management, which took place in 1984 in Versailles, and then at the second conference in 1991 in Rotterdam. These events brought together regulatory agencies and industrial producers worldwide and contributed enormously to a measure of common understanding. I think particularly of the second one, at which my speech followed an impassioned but vague manifesto delivered by a representative of one of the environmental groups. I was able to table Noranda's first-published annual environmental report, which detailed exactly how we perceived the problems and how we'd moved to address them. No other company in attendance had managed to produce this sort of document, and I think our actions set a new tone for the conference. Certainly I was asked to send out many copies.

Under Frank's guidance Noranda also established its own environmental-audit regime. This procedure is both comprehensive and objective; there are something like eighty-five auditors who cover the group of associated companies by forming teams of two or three and examining facilities with which they have no direct connection. It works in theory and in practice, and I recommend it to anyone who wants to get a true environmental reading of their operations.

One or two other examples of Noranda's environmental programs must suffice to show the range of difficulties we encountered and overcame. Any mining or smelting site produces large quantities of tailings, the ground-up residue that remains after copper, zinc, gold, or other metals have been extracted from their ores. Tailings often contain traces of substances like arsenic and acidic compounds used to extract these minerals. It's hard to get rid of them, so the goal is to render them harmless and, if possible, less unsightly. Noranda spent a lot of time and money developing better methods of impounding the tailings. Finally, after consulting with agricultural researchers at the University of Guelph, we and others came up with grass-and-legume mixtures that would grow — indeed, thrive — atop the tailings ponds.

The other trick with tailings is to make sure they don't escape and contaminate the surrounding area. One of the largest sites we had to deal with was also among the most sensitive, because of its position. The Brenda molybdenum-copper mine near Peachland, B.C., sat on a low mountain slope from which water ran down into the fruit farms of the Okanagan Valley. There was no margin for error, so a series of dams was devised that worked on the fail-safe principle. There were three containment dams and three separate treatment plants ready to capture whatever liquid might conceivably overflow. This cost many millions, but it worked.

A second environmentally sensitive project, because of its vast size, was the Hemlo Camp in northern Ontario, where three gold mines came into production almost simultaneously. Here we were on solid ground — it's always easier to build new than to retrofit an older facility, as anyone who's had occasion to renovate a house will attest. In the case of Hemlo, Queen's Park had the wisdom to adopt the so-called one-window approach; thus a single provincial government department was responsible for supervising the entire construction process, approving and issuing all necessary permits. Environmental guidelines were crystal clear from the start, which meant that the companies involved could cost out the requisite procedures and include them in their calculations from day one. Everyone knew and understood the rules going in, the best technology available was economically implementable, and above all there was a willingness on all sides to work together in a constructive manner.

Compared with its mining sites, Noranda's forest operations were fraught with controversy and marked by mounting confrontation. Canadians love trees, and so hate the idea of cutting them down, even to provide a million-odd jobs and furnish society with countless products it couldn't do without. There's majesty in a towering forest grove; it's a potent image that cannot fail to evoke an emotional response, whereas the average mine is a hole in the middle of nowhere.

Noranda Forest's first environmental set-to occurred in the 1960s during construction of the Northwood pulp mill near Prince George, B.C. This was the period when brand-new facilities were springing up across the country, all designed to use the partial logs and wood chips that had previously been burned or left to rot. Stringent standards were formulated by both the federal and provincial governments, which at the time were still talking to each other. Northwood strongly supported these guidelines, which its new mill met with room to spare. Indeed, it was recognized as the most advanced and clean-running facility in all the Pacific Northwest. Perhaps in celebration, the plant manager took a group of admiring photographers down to the outflow pipe and drank a cupful of the mill's effluent, which gesture — though certainly dramatic — seemed above and beyond the call of duty.

In the 1970s fresh troubles surrounding the twin bogies of clear-cut logging and dioxin discharge loomed. Noranda found itself on the firing line almost at once, because it had taken over MacMillan Bloedel, which for years had held logging rights to Meares Island in Clayoquot Sound on the west coast of Vancouver Island. Meares is the subject of a native land claim and is in full view of Tofino, a popular tourist destination. In late 1979, as part of a five-year management plan, MacMillan Bloedel announced its intention to begin harvesting on Meares. A small portion had been logged seven years previously with no objections raised. Indeed, there had once been an exploratory mineral operation on the island. Now, however, the pendulum had swung back. The provincial government withheld approval of MacMillan Bloedel's plan until Meares was taken out of the equation.

Never mind that many of its trees were overmature, decaying, dying, or dead, and that the plan called for culling only one-sixtieth of the island's forests a year. All logging ceased. The environmentalists were quick to realize what could be accomplished if sufficient pressure was brought to bear, and they moved to escalate a struggle that continues unabated to this day.

In 1988 MacMillan Bloedel calculated that environmental groups of one stripe or another were demanding the cessation of logging in sixteen percent of its timberlands in the Alberni region of Vancouver Island. Opposition to our activities throughout the West Coast temperate rain forest was no longer local, regional, or provincial; it was global.

As the head of Noranda Forest, I soon became accustomed to being cast as the heavy in some far-reaching conspiracy, or as an apologist for an environmentally reprehensible industry that was bent on creating a wasteland up and down the province by wantonly destroying the last great untouched stands of virgin timber. Fresh charges and countercharges flew as protests became more frequent and far more confrontational.

To explore fully the ramifications of this debate would make this book a weighty doorstop indeed. Let me touch upon one or two high points.

First, and most obviously, you can't make money from a wasteland. No one wants a healthy productive forest more than a forest company. If nothing else, enlightened self-interest dictates that we do all we can to ensure a continuing supply, because our livelihood depends on it. Second, our ability to do business depends also on public consent. A resource company can operate only with the permission of the provincial government, which owns the vast majority of the forest. The government, in turn, answers to the actual landlords, who are its citizens.

The truth is that at least twenty percent of Vancouver Island's big trees are preserved forever in national and provincial parks and other set-aside areas. Stands of timber that have been logged and replanted in the Queen Charlotte Islands are indistinguishable from the natural forest. In any case, projected harvesting in "old-growth" forests — the definition of which varies — represents less than two percent of total forest activity nationwide.

Another flashpoint of the environmental debate is the thorny issue of clear-cutting. I could defend clear-cutting till the cows come home, pointing out that it mimics nature's own forest fires, from which the forests have recovered quite nicely since time immemorial. I could state the obvious — that forestry isn't a cottage industry, that selective, tree-by-tree cuts are uneconomical and won't support a local workforce. It's true that when an area is logged, it's often replanted with a single species, but that doesn't slow nature down; many locations soon display a fair measure of diversity. Besides, if you don't like harvesting and replenishing with a monoculture in the forest, how do you feel about a wheat field? And so on and so on. I wouldn't be able to convince you in a million years — because the morning-after shot of a clear-cut is ugly.

What irks the most is the environmentalists' treasured tenet that clear-cutting be abolished tomorrow. If your position is absolute — all or nothing and damn the consequences — you're going to wind up with next to nothing, and the consequences won't be to your taste. Cut size has already been greatly reduced, largely in response to public pressure, but we aren't going to stop clear-cutting, unless of course we're ordered to by the provinces, which will only happen when competing jurisdictions do the same. Such a scenario would be interesting to behold. The forest industry will go in and take every twenty-third tree; we'll harvest with hand saws and teams of oxen, if those are the conditions that are placed upon us. There won't be much of an industry left, and consumers will be stunned by the prices they'll have to pay for paper towels, two-by-fours, and furniture, but ideological purity will have won the day.

It's easy to remain unsullied at a distance, and some of forestry's most vocal detractors have never set foot in the woods. It's all very well to sit in an urban office tower and proclaim the virtues of an allegedly pristine wilderness. If you happen to live in proximity to that wilderness, and your living depends on its forests or mineral wealth, then you may hold a slightly different view. Over and over again I've found that, if people actually visit a forest operation, their minds change when they are presented with hard evidence of the way industry conducts itself. The majority of the charges — that forest operators have been insensitive to problems of overallocation and overcutting, and opposed to sustained-yield allocation and prompt reforestation — are demonstrably untrue.

In 1980 Canada's major forestry firms, together with the International Woodworkers of America, established the Canadian Forest Congress. This was a landmark attempt to involve all the stakeholders — including environmentalists, native groups, and tourism operators — in efforts to assess the condition of forests nationwide and to plan for the future. Industry and workers, not governments and environmentalists, were the guiding force, as well they had to be. In fact the provincial governments had been, to a degree, imprudent and indifferent. The allocations they'd granted to the new pulp mills of the 1960s had proved to be insufficient to support sustained-yield practices, and the Canadian Forest Congress was the first to point this out.

Since 1980 what we call "not satisfactorily restocked" areas of the Canadian forest have been steadily diminishing. During that period, seedlings planted have risen from 250 million to almost one billion a year. Nothing is perfect, but on balance, no better forestry is being generally practised anywhere in the world.

Another flashpoint in the environmental debate is the pulp-mill effluent, dioxin, which is produced during chlorine bleaching. Dioxins and furans are actually a group of 210 slightly different chlorinated compounds. In high concentrations, they're labelled toxic. Exactly how toxic remains open to question.

Until the 1950s any concentration of dioxins lower than one part per million was considered to be zero — thus perfectly safe. By 1965, however, dioxins could be detected in parts per billion. On this scale one part translates to sixteen inches in the distance to the moon. Eventually scientists, armed with ever more sophisticated and sensitive equipment, were busily searching for parts per trillion. To grasp the concept of one part per trillion, think about a single second in 30,000 years. Not surprisingly dioxins started popping up in more and more places than had previously been suspected.

Actually dioxins have been around for quite a while. They exist, for example, in wood. We know this, because they're present in unbleached pulp as well. In addition, they're produced during the combustion of any materials, including all fossil fuels, that contain chlorine atoms. Thus huge quantities are emitted by forest fires, by municipal incinerators, and by the family car.

A modern mill might, in the course of 300,000 tonnes of production, emit an amount of dioxin the size of a sugar cube. In fact, all of Canada's mills together accounted, during the 1990s, for only five percent of total dioxins created annually. You might not choose to ingest a cube of dioxin, but you'll never have to. The only creatures who have are laboratory rats, which received massive doses and not surprisingly suffered a number of adverse effects. The same results were not observed in hamsters. Dioxin's only verifiable effect on humans is known as chloracne — in other words, bad skin — a critical condition only if you're a teenager looking for a date. A person would have to drink thirty-two Olympic-size swimming pools of the stuff before developing a mildly annoying rash.

And yet, a move away from chlorine bleaching began, first in Germany, spurred by the Green political party. Soon it spread to Scandinavia, then to North America. By the late 1980s dioxin had become synonymous with Agent Orange, the defoliant used by the U.S. military during the Vietnam War. By 1990 it was routinely referred to as "the deadliest substance known to science," a distinction previously held by PCBs.

No one can handle that sort of opprobrium, and research establish-ments throughout the industry were working overtime to isolate the problem and arrive at practical solutions. These were implemented, production methods were altered, concentrations were found to be well within allowable levels, and it became clear that there'd never been much cause for worry. Because of a lack of mutually agreed-upon data, a great deal of time and money — by some estimates, billions of dollars worldwide — had been allocated to curing what was in essence a nonproblem. Admittedly some pulp producers, including Sodra in Sweden, announced that they would get out of the chlorine-bleaching business altogether. MacMillan Bloedel did not. Both these decisions were predicated on customer demand.

A final environmental issue relating to the forest industry is recycling, to which no one can object. Consumers of forest products are perhaps more wasteful than those of any other resource. The throwaway society has made expendable packaging into an art form. Who wouldn't be pleased to see the end of bags within bags within bags, not to mention the daily avalanche of unwanted junk mail? The trouble is that the public, unable to shoot the messenger and unwilling to examine its own behaviour, has striven to hold the producers responsible. (Imagine a glass manufacturer being hounded into insolvency because end users toss bottles by the roadside.) At least we now have the missing piece of the puzzle that's always curtailed a massive recycling effort: a workable collection system. Assured of a supply of recyclable paper products, industry responded with regional recycling plants. Nowadays, of course, the majority of packaging, newspapers, and stationery contains a degree of secondary fibre. Municipalities used to pay $20 a tonne to have cast-off news-paper hauled away. Now a tonne brings as much as $150 on the open market and is at risk of being poached in the middle of the night by scavengers. Indeed, the industry is faced with what may yet become a constrained supply. Still, there are limits to recycling growth. Some people imagine that all you have to do is heave a load of newsprint into a vat and it comes out clean. Not quite; the process is expensive and complex. The quantities involved are also problematic in the extreme. At one point it was estimated that, in order to reach the target of thirty-percent recycled newsprint, we'd have to collect every single shred from every city and town in the country, then import an extra two million tonnes.

And what of industry's strained relations with the environmental movement? I can best illustrate this by talking about two men, one of whom you will most certainly recognize. The other, and in my estimation the real leader, is less well-known.

The first is broadcaster and activist David Suzuki. Suzuki is without doubt a charismatic personality who's done much to advance the nation's environmental consciousness — not to mention his own celebrity status. I honour the office — we need people to stir things up — but not, on occasion, the man. I have grave reservations about many of his more extreme statements, which don't hold water, pristine or otherwise. Nor does he let the facts stand in the way of a good story. I've seen him hold forth on television on the plight of whales in one particular location, meanwhile standing at an entirely different site. He's often the victim of his own rhetoric, which does him and his causes no credit.

David and I have exchanged a lively and frequently acrimonious correspondence for many years. He tolerates me, I believe, because he likes my wife and daughters. Indeed, his foundation supports my daughter's sustainable-development project in the Amazon. We met when we were both members of the Science Council of Canada. It was a case of distrust at first sight, on his part at least. As time went by, he came to view me as less of an environmental dinosaur, and we became friends — so much so that I returned home one night to find him, a Brazilian Indian chief, songwriter Gordon Lightfoot, and a rather baffled contingent of my corporate peers, all standing around the front room, drinking my liquor. This unusual group had been invited at the urging of my daughter Barbara.

David, to give him his due, is surely Canada's best-known apostle
of environmental causes. He has a remarkable following and equally
remarkable personal charm; he's truly a Pied Piper. Once we were
walking down the street together in Ottawa, and little kids ran up to
touch his hand. None of these children would recognize a Canadian
corporate leader if he bit them, and if they did happen to identify a
captain of industry he'd be more likely to get a snowball in the ear
than a pat on the back.

I'd like to salute another member of industry's loyal opposition,
Monte Hummel, the president of World Wildlife Canada. We first
met when the Noranda executive sat down in our boardroom for full
and frank discussions with Pollution Probe, of which Monte was a
founder. This group was widely seen at the time to be a collection of
radical barn-burners who were interested only in reshaping the
world overnight in conformity with rules of their own making, but
Monte, on the contrary, seemed to be a person we could reason with.

Later he went on to World Wildlife, which I was invited to join as
trustee during Doug Bassett's tenure as chairman. This invitation was
perhaps an effort to set up a sort of dynamic tension within the group,
but it struck me as a very forward-looking move. I accepted with
pleasure, and the whole experience has proved to be rewarding and
delightful. I've always claimed to be an environmentalist who chooses
to work for change from the inside. Monte and I may have our differences, but he's never failed to respect my standpoints and embrace
me personally, which stands as testimony to his breadth of mind.

Monte's larger view stems from the fact that, although he has his
passions, he's also a professionally trained forester with a fair grasp of
what goes on in the real world. This was demonstrated when he
attended one of the meetings I convened with Noranda's senior
managers nationwide. I'd primed the pump by giving them copies
of a book titled *Where Have All the Birds Gone?* by biologist John
Terborgh, which painted a clear picture of how species diminish and
disappear. Monte commanded their respect because he didn't try to

fast-talk or fake his way through the session. Instead, he mounted a well-reasoned defence of his Endangered Spaces program, which identifies areas of unique ecological significance, then sets aside twelve percent of them for parkland or permanent conservation. This has been a great success in B.C., and industry in general views it as a desirable and practical compromise.

Monte was also responsible for organizing yet another initiative, World Wildlife's Toxicology program. Noranda covers the basic administration costs, and the federal government matches the contributions of other industry members on a dollar-for-dollar basis. This works well and has produced a number of significant and useful studies.

Monte is ably supported by his wife, a committed environmental journalist, just as I'm prodded on ecological topics by the Zimmerman tribe. Activists were nothing new to me. As I've said, I had four of them — five, counting my wife — staring me down at mealtimes. All my children developed an environmental awareness, each in his or her own way. The fact that I was first a parent, then a grandparent, naturally encouraged me to give thought to the future of the human race.

So I do, as does everyone else, but what's required to shape both thought and action is reliable research and data. Certain environmental "hazards" may indeed be life-threatening, while others are innocuous. But each one, no matter how serious or frivolous, must be fully understood before it can be acted upon, taken out of the equation, or subjected to further examination.

For example, daughter Barbara worked for many years on a World Wildlife project in the Amazon, which was trying to establish a "minimum ecological reserve" — an area left undisturbed adjacent to one that was actively logged. No comparable study has ever been conducted in Canada. No Canadian environmental organization has ever taken an objective scientific look at a tract of woodland before and after it's logged. Nor has a Canadian forest company, to the industry's shame. Small-scale studies have been done in places such as New Brunswick's Fundy National Forest and in several provincial parks, but these locations see very little in the way of logging activity. (I know what you're asking: why didn't Noranda go ahead and do a unilateral study? Had we done so, we'd probably have been denounced as self-serving. If we'd slipped up in any particular, if our methodology had been even slightly deficient, the resulting criticism would have set the idea back twenty years.)

I maintain that the best-managed forests are privately held, but Canadian forests are largely owned by the provinces, which set up able and committed forestry departments, then starve them of needed budgets in favour of vote-buying schemes elsewhere. Stumpage payments disappear into general revenues, rather than being directed back into silviculture. Every year more and more tracts of forest are withdrawn from commercial exploitation so as to create protected areas and parks. We're shrinking the base, and unless we're careful the nation's forests will not be able to support the value society places on them.

I've seen any number of environment ministers come and go, having announced, the day they were sworn in, that a new Eden was around the corner. Few had the slightest idea what they were talking about. Oddly enough, one of the most effective people to hold the federal portfolio was Lucien Bouchard, but he left his post before he could do much good. The best one of all was Jean Charest, who really did his homework. Others, including many in the provinces, have been useless in the extreme. All too often, when governments go charging off in pursuit of a new environmental grail, their actions are counterproductive — for three reasons. First, progress is impeded, because the industry doesn't know what it's supposed to progress toward. Second, false hopes are aroused among the public, who then succumb to cynicism when Utopia doesn't arrive within the week. Third, the people who know the most and are truly striving to make things work in environmentally acceptable ways are demeaned and insulted by those who should — but never seem to — know better.

What is needed is a forum for fair hearings, a stock of unassailable data, a more comprehensive analysis by the media, and any number of more reasonable, less heated discussions. Governments attempt to resolve these disagreements, but they are driven by the need to appear politically correct. Plus, they're chronically unprepared and not fully empowered to act. It's my belief that a solution exists to many if not all these issues, but is overlooked. Instead, things reach emotional fever pitch, and industry, at least, is forced to spend time and money doing the unnecessary and disputing the untrue.

Over the years I've tried to put a little bit of what I see as the truth on record. I've said to countless audiences that forestry firms in particular should be saluted as exemplars of environmentally sound behaviour. They produce no waste that goes untreated or remains unaccounted for. They have to — they're closely watched, quantified on a daily basis, and regulated into the ground. A pulp mill may smell a little bit, but that's about the extent of it. It emits an effluent that's drinkable and virtually undetectable twenty kilometres downstream and does no harm along the way. I invite you to come by for a visit sometime. You'll be astounded by what you see.

And what part have you, the reader, played in the environmental struggle lately? Yes, you recycle, when you remember to. Yes, you turn off the office lights at night to conserve electricity. But chances are that in the summertime you light up the barbecue. In winter you enjoy sitting in front of a fireplace. You drive a car all year round. Well, a backyard grill emits proportionately more dioxin than does a pulp mill. The average North American car, driven 20,000 kilometres a year, releases its own weight in carbon into the atmosphere. The *Exxon Valdez* oil spill in Alaska's William Sound amounted to more than 150 million gallons of oil, which certainly qualifies as an environmental catastrophe, but even more frightening is the fact that 200 million gallons of used crankcase oil are surreptitiously and illegally dumped into ditches and storm sewers every year. And recreational boaters, who should surely be concerned about water quality, jettison an estimated 100,000 tonnes of plastic litter into offshore and inland waters every season. Imagine your delight if someone lurked outside your house each week to audit your garbage and imposed or threatened sanctions if you slipped an orange-juice tin into the trash bag. That's what industry faces every day. Imagine the response of your elected representatives — for example, a city council — if they were zapped with massive fines because they discharged untreated municipal wastes. A sizeable number of Canadian cities and towns are back in the Dark Ages when it comes to effluent. If an industry did anything comparable, it would be shut down within the hour and all their top management hanged from the highest yardarm.

I'm the first to admit that industry isn't without fault. There'll always be pirates and fly-by-nighters, but logic says they can't get away with it in the heavily regulated resource field. Some will comply grudgingly, hewing to the letter, not the spirit, of the law. Most companies are members of industry associations that have voluntarily established environmental codes, and most have appointed senior environmental officers, made environmental audits of principal sites, and ensured that reports are regularly presented, either to an environmental committee of the board of directors or directly to the board itself. All these measures ought to be applauded, but I've seen very little public recognition of the fact that industry has adopted them.

There is absolutely no question that industry recognizes its environmental responsibilities in a way unheard of twenty, ten, or even five years ago. Just as the freewheeling financial markets of the 1930s led to Securities Commissions and revised Corporations Acts, generally accepted accounting principles, and the like, the environmental battles of the 1970s and 1980s have resulted in the need for a regulatory framework. Environmentalists have won the battle, and they would now do well to join forces with industry instead of squandering their resources opposing it. Environmentalism is everyone's business, everyone's responsibility. The solutions to the problems that face us all today can and will be resolved to everyone's lasting benefit. No one today would seriously defend what served for far too long as the status quo. The challenge is to formulate together what will become the new realities of tomorrow.

7

Living With the Fourth Estate

I'm not much of a gambler, but I'd have won a bundle over the years if I had bet that every time the media did a story on Canada's forest industry, the same two images were guaranteed to appear on your television screen or in the pages of newspapers and magazines. The first is a pulp mill belching clouds of smoke. The second is what we call a cut-over block, a patch of timber immediately after logging.

What you see emitting from the "smokestack" is in fact ninety-nine percent vaporized distilled water. It may look ominous and it may stink, but it is entirely benign. Nevertheless, the viewer's instinctive reaction is: there go those goddamn pulp mills again, fouling the atmosphere, screwing up the ozone layer, and inflicting on us all a blight of heavy-industrial smog whose long-term carcinogenic effects we can only dimly imagine.

Similarly, a cut-over block is not a pretty sight. Every tree has been mown down and it looks as if nothing will ever grow there again, as if most of the wildlife has retreated into the neighbouring forest cover never to return. But stop and think: what's going on just out of camera range? If the camera panned to left or right, you'd see how small the cut-over block is in relation to the surrounding countryside. From ground level you wouldn't be able to see the next such block, because the blocks have been laid out in a pattern across the landscape. Green corridors have been left intact; the birds and mammals have free passage and do quite nicely once the noise dies down. Debris has been mulched and left in place. Soon another crew will begin replanting healthy young seedlings, and the growing stock will be maintained, if not enhanced.

I have a bone or two to pick with the media, because I've experienced this kind of selective, biased reporting time and time again. I find it ironic whenever a newspaper goes on the anti–forest industry warpath — a case of biting the mills that feed it. The resource industries have always come under intensive scrutiny, and rightly so. They operate on public land, they're often the biggest or only game in town, they trade across the world, they have a major impact on the environment, the jobs they provide are numerous, arduous and at times dangerous, and the workforce is heavily unionized. In short they can be relied on to cough up a story any day of the week.

At various points in my career I have been misquoted, misrepresented, and occasionally maligned. My comments have been truncated, compressed, childishly oversimplified, turned upside down, and yanked light-years out of context. But I am one of the lucky ones. The media were generally fair with me — perhaps because I was usually frank with them and took the trouble to help them get the story straight. I never went out of my way to court the media, but I treated journalists with respect, and they usually returned the favour. They had their job to do, I had mine, and we never, to my recollection, came to serious verbal blows. Besides, they weren't picking on me personally. Anyone who is engaged in any form of business activity views the fourth estate's attentions with a mixture of anticipation (most people like to see their names in print) and alarm (odds are the story will be to some extent a distortion of reality).

The media wield considerable power, but they have a short attention span. They are drawn inexorably to the next assignment. If they keelhaul you on Friday, rest assured they'll find someone else by the time Saturday's deadline rolls around. You can't go to the wall on every instance of what strikes you as incomplete or slanted reporting. It's not wise to plant the idea that you have nothing better to do with your time than to read the newspapers and/or watch the news. This was one of the knocks on Mulroney — he was obsessed by what the media had to say about him. People suspected that, once he'd checked out all the editorial pages, it was time to go for lunch, which is no way to run a country.

But there are some things you can't let pass. Blatant inaccuracies and downright lies can and must be refuted one way or another; otherwise, they lodge in the permanent record and come back to haunt you. Turn the other cheek, and you'll be blindsided again and again.

Lump enough highly charged antibusiness images together over time, and they're bound to make their mark. Even just a single story can make a company's workers feel resentful, suspicious, and ashamed, or alienate the community where its plant or mill is located. An attack on a single firm can cast doubt on an entire sector; there's one bad apple, so let's peel the rest of them just to make sure.

Media reporting is a crucible in which public opinion is formed, and public opinion has a long shelf life. It contributes to the formation of public policy, which ought to be established on the most reasonable bases possible — sound logic based on hard facts, not knee-jerk reactions to fabricated crises. Media coverage catches the fleeting attention of our elected representatives. It drives the politicians, who drive the bureaucrats, who then drive business to distraction with overregulation. The interplay of business and media should be part of an ongoing process that involves public knowledge, public education, and representation to the public of a business point of view.

When we talk about "the media," we often do ourselves and the media's several components a disservice. It's simplistic to assert that "the media" are antibusiness. They, too, are businesses, although they are often hypocritical about admitting it; they'll defend someone else's downtrodden workers till the cows come home, but listen to them holler when they're on the wrong side of a picket line.

Today's media owners may decry the sins of "big business," but if you want a crash course in hegemony, take a quick look at the nearest newspaper empire. Until quite recently the press barons have been far more adept at making and hanging on to money than many of their peers. On average newspaper profits for the past forty-odd years have been nearly double those in the natural-resources field. Rates of return have at times reached fifteen and even twenty percent.

One reason media profits are so high is that journalists' salaries are shamefully low. As a general rule the most senior and able magazine editor makes a fraction of what his or her opposite number (in terms of experience and responsibility) would command in fields such as advertising and public relations. Ageing scribes yearn for the day when they can rack up enough clippings to become professors of journalism. A reluctance on the media owners' part to spend money on hiring, training, and supporting quality staff does much to produce mediocre or superficial coverage. This is not, I hasten to stress, the reporters' fault. Unless we're talking about a specialized business publication or a major newspaper's business section, a reporter is quite probably ill-equipped to comprehend and convey the larger issues behind a given story, simply because he or she hasn't been given sufficient resources or time to do so. In the world of the media, as everywhere else, you get what you pay for.

Certainly we made our mistakes, and the Tasmanian effort was one of them. Another incident comes to mind which at least taught a major lesson.

In 1983 life was not so hot for the resource industries. We couldn't turn a profit to save our souls; the cupboard was bare and getting barer. Meanwhile, labour negotiations loomed, and the unions were out for what I considered to be inordinate wage increases. So I decided to write to the publishers of the *Vancouver Sun*, the Vancouver *Province*, the *Prince George Citizen*, and the *Kamloops News* to explain Noranda's position. These letters were personal and (or so I assumed) off the record. I said that the forest industry had been zapped by the recession, had taken crippling losses, and was therefore forced to adopt a hard line on costs. I also said I sensed that Noranda's workforce, given an absolutely free choice, might take a ten- or fifteen-percent wage cut if by doing so they could secure their jobs. I stressed that no one in management had suggested this, even though I was convinced that the stance taken by the union leaders was not representative of their membership. I enclosed with my letters copies of an internal report Noranda had prepared from publicly available data that laid out our affairs in some detail and contrasted our situation with those of our competitors. I added that the industry as a whole was bleeding red ink. Noranda was the biggest loser only because we were the biggest player. The report, I said, could be made available as background to the newspapers' editors in hopes it might prove useful in reporting or reflecting on the negotiations as they got under way.

Then I made the mistake of going to Europe for a stretch. While I was away, the *Vancouver Sun* called my office and asked to use the letter in an article. One of my staff members ill-advisedly gave the okay, and a piece appeared under the headline "Job Security for Pay Cuts Suggested." My thought that the workforce "might" take a cut had been changed by the reporter early on in the piece to read "would probably," although that specific paragraph of my letter, complete with the *correct* quote, was printed verbatim farther down in the piece. To add insult to injury, the *Sun* ran a photo of me with the caption "appeals to newspaper."

As if that wasn't bad enough, the *Sun* had also read my letter to all the usual suspects to elicit their responses. The president of the Canadian Paperworkers Union termed my comments "crude and cruel." The effect of the article, which appeared just as the bargaining process was beginning, may be imagined, as may my mood, when I got wind of what had happened. No lasting harm was done to the negotiations, but the article's publication made me look stupid — which I may have been in imagining that the tone of my covering letters and the fact that they and the reports had been sent directly to the publishers established that my intent was to provide background information only. The lesson of this sorry little tale? There's no such thing as "off the record." Remember the caution issued by the British police: anything you say may be taken down and used in evidence. The story does serve as an antidote to those who believe that corporate power and influence guarantee good press. As it happened, the *Vancouver Sun* was a Southam newspaper, and at that time I was a Southam director!

WITH OVER TWO DECADES SPENT as a media-appointed "industry spokesperson" and occasionally as an unwitting straw man on forestry environmental issues, I have distilled my experience in dealing with our beloved fourth estate into some universal precepts for the edification of other businesspeople who find themselves in the often unwelcome glare of the media's spotlight. In my not altogether humble view, those executives who choose to disregard this advice will almost certainly live to regret their decision by the time the six o'clock news rolls around.

Zimmerman's Eight Commandments: A Lesson in Dealing With the Media

1. *Give succinct answers.* If a journalist poses a question, it is your

job to communicate your response clearly. Don't blame the reporter if he or she muddies what you say if you say it in a way no one can understand. Stay on topic: if someone in your New Brunswick subsidiary has been caught skimming funds, the reporter will not be open to a discussion of everything your firm has done in the way of ethics seminars. Remember: your answer will always be sliced and diced to the bone in the editing process, so it had better contain the nub of what you intend to say.

2. *Never presuppose a warm reception.* Reporters are paid to be sceptical; the reader or viewer is at best neutral, waiting to be convinced. Don't be misled by your success in the boardroom or on the speakers' circuit. What wows the converted cuts no ice with the disinterested or antagonistic viewer.

3. *Tell the truth, the whole truth, and nothing but the truth,* leaving out only what can legitimately be classed as confidential. The media can't be fooled or hoodwinked. They can spot you treading water and sense when you're talking straight. You shouldn't have to fake it, because you know more about your business than they do, but don't expect they're going to accept what you say holus bolus. If you want a cheering section, hire one. If you want to make motherhood statements, rent a billboard. You aren't in a popularity contest. What you want is serious, professional fair play.

4. *Know your reporter as an adversary and keep your guard up.* Every reporter who interviews you has an attitude; outlaw journalist Hunter S. Thompson once said that the only example of journalistic objectivity he ever bumped into was the anti-shoplifting surveillance camera in Woody Creek, Colorado. A good reporter admits his or her prejudices and will try to keep them out of a story. Pundits or commentators won't; they're

being paid to mouth off, to fit you into their take on things. Your job is to know whom you are dealing with and govern yourself accordingly. Be informed about a commentator's slant and a newspaper's editorial policy and traditional political allegiance. As you build a relationship with the media, you keep tabs on one another. You have few excuses for being caught napping. I shudder when businesspeople claim they've been sandbagged by the press. Quite frankly, if you can be entrapped or tripped up by a reporter, maybe you deserve it.

5. *Be available*. Reporters don't call you for want of something better to do. They want a story. If you don't provide it, they'll turn to your competitors or to the person or group on the other side of a given issue. Enlightened self-interest tells you that you can run but you can't hide. For example, when Noranda was attempting its takeover of MacMillan Bloedel, we were in competition with British Columbia Resources Investment Company (BCRIC), which let its public-relations department carry the ball. Their press releases were murky and uninformative, their president unforthcoming to the media. The day we announced our takeover bid I was in Toronto attending a board meeting, where I remained locked up for four or five hours. When I came out, it was late in the day, but my desk was piled high with messages from media people in B.C. I sat down and started returning calls. It took me until seven-fifteen at night, saying much the same things over and over again. Simply because I took the time personally to make those calls, I inadvertently won the public-relations battle. I don't attribute our successful bid to the fact that I did so; I wasn't dialling for dollars. I acted out of common courtesy — somebody phones you, you know it's about something you want correctly portrayed, so you phone them back. The B.C. media got the story straight from the "forest baron's" mouth, and it paid off in

the transition period after our bid had been accepted. Noranda wasn't cut all that much slack, but at least the company wasn't vilified for the acquisition.

6. *Get it right the first time.* Activists, protesters, and industry critics can get away with all kinds of wild accusations and factual distortions, but Lord pity the business spokesperson who gets his facts wrong. His errors or omissions will be immediately seized upon as evidence of a plot or a coverup. Space will be made for the story in the front section of the daily paper, the public's worst fears will be reconfirmed, and the big bad capitalist will have been caught acting according to type. Not what you'd call a level playing field, but your only protection is getting the facts straight.

7. *Do not get baited into playing their game!* If the media, broadly speaking, are prone to advancing the environmental agenda and arguably the labour agenda, as well, you've got to grin and bear it. You may think it's only fair to toss around a couple of wild and baseless charges of your own, say, that ninety-two percent of all labour leaders steal sheep, or that a daily dose of dioxin improves one's sex life.

Resist the temptation to sling your own mud. It's not a matter of standing on some imagined dignity. Business, I believe, has got to behave responsibly; we are, or ought to be, the grown-ups. In the case of a fractious labour dispute, it's your duty and responsibility to make a deal that everyone can live with. In the case of an environmental standoff, the onus is on you to analyse and remedy the problem. Friends of the Spotted Owl don't have to go out there the next day and do something about managing the forest or keep thousands of people employed.

The media can be counted on to show (almost nightly these days) a shuffling band of protesters, chanting, "Hey, hey, ho, ho!

So-and-so has got to go!" — a rallying cry that seems to suit every occasion. No one bothers to point out that the protest is fruitless, because So-and-so isn't going anywhere. If he or she did in fact go, then who would fill the gap? Not the protesters, who are incapable of doing so. Indeed, if So-and-so's opponents are luckless enough to assume power, they'll be faced with the same shuffling band, chanting the same nihilistic slogan. And yet the cameras are out there like clockwork. Business cannot play these and other silly-bugger games, because it has more to lose. So, when it comes to getting the job done — a job that, for better or worse, may include getting your words or photograph in the papers or on the news — you have to be right and go about it the right way.

8. *Know when to shut up.* A favourite ploy among business's adversaries is to make some wild and baseless charge that you must then deny. Suppose that someone calls you a fascist. This makes your blood boil, and you tell the media in no uncertain terms that you're not. The next day's headline is sure to read: "I'm No Fascist, Irate Pillar of Industry Claims." The accuser (who was previously less well-known than you, so that smearing you was his best hope of getting some ink) has thus achieved several aims at once. He's diverted attention from the real issue, whatever that may be; added validity to his accusation (you've been goaded into an angry response); succeeded in getting a double hit on his slander; and planted the suspicion among credulous media consumers that you're indeed a fascist who doth protest too much. The public believes that where there's smoke there's fire, so don't get snookered into fanning the flames.

Thus endeth the lesson.

8

Bedevilled in Tasmania

Noranda's misadventures in Tasmania came about through a tangled series of events that handily demonstrate how bad press and bad politics often go hand in hand. The Commonwealth of Australia consists of six states and two territories. The federal capital is Canberra, located on the mainland. The state of Tasmania is composed of a large island (Tasmania proper) about 250 kilometres offshore, along with several smaller islands that stretch almost 1,400 kilometres out to sea. Its capital is Hobart, and relations between the two regimes are often less than smooth. Australians tend to look upon Tasmania as a sort of verdant Newfoundland. Their attitude is a mixture of envy and scorn — nice scenery, but the natives are a touch backward. For their part, Tasmanians refer to Australia as the North Island.

Tasmania is indeed very beautiful; its central plateau is heavily forested and studded with alpine lakes. These forests include more than five hundred species of the eucalyptus tree, the leaves and shoots of which form the staple diet of the koala. Both Tasmania and Australia have plenty of eucalyptus, to the benefit of the koalas and the timber industry, because eucalyptus is a valuable and fast-growing hardwood. Australia's forest-products industry is the nation's second-largest, surpassed only by agriculture. It employs directly well over 100,000 people. As in Canada, more than two-thirds of all natural-growth forests and tree plantations are on public lands. These holdings provide the vast majority of hardwood sawlogs and wood chips. Unfortunately Australia lacks both domestic softwoods and the market pulping facilities that would enable it to process excess chips. Instead, the chips are exported in large quantities, mainly to Japan.

In 1989, when our story unfolds, these shipments brought about $430-million annually, but Australia then had to turn around and import $495-million worth of softwood timber, as well as an additional $1.2-billion worth of pulp-and-paper products. The latter sums accounted for thirteen percent of the country's trade imbalance and represented by far the largest component of its foreign debt. (At the time, the Canadian and Australian currencies were more or less at par, so the dollar figures in this story are equivalent between the two countries.)

Ever since 1961 a firm called North Broken Hill Pty. had been operating, through its subsidiary, Associated Pulp and Paper Mills, a particle-board-and-paper complex at Wesley Vale, as well as a paper mill at nearby Burnie. This stretch of Tasmania's northern coast is well-known for its productive farmland, but few objections had been raised to the existing plants. The board mill was small-scale, the newer paper mill unobtrusive, and the older one at Burnie part of the landscape. The company produced a far greater quantity of chips than it could use, and these were exported to Japan. North Broken Hill was a large and highly diversified corporation, one of very few

142

worldwide that embraced, as did Noranda, both mining and forestry. It wanted to expand these plants and had been negotiating with Robin Gray, Tasmania's premier, to obtain a licence that would allow the company to chip more wood. But Gray had hopes of value-added processing somewhere down the line and had stymied North Broken Hill's attempts at piecemeal improvements.

In the late 1980s world markets expressed increased demand for chemically bleached white eucalyptus pulp, to be used in the production of tissues and printing paper. Sensing a window of opportunity, North Broken Hill decided to build a bleached-kraft pulp mill at the Wesley Vale site to utilize its excess chips, as well as quantities of the fast-growing eucalyptus. Premier Gray, in turn, drove a hard bargain on forest royalties and fibre supply, forcing North Broken Hill to commit to purchase wood from government holdings at a price that was two to three times the prevailing rates elsewhere. This precedent led Gray to believe that North Broken Hill could be pushed around, that all of its subsequent bargaining positions could be improved upon.

In 1987, quite by chance, I happened to entertain Peter Wade, the managing director of North Broken Hill, who was paying a courtesy visit to Toronto. During our dinner conversation he mentioned that he was seeking a partner, because his firm, while dominant in mining, wasn't big enough to assume the project's full financial risk. Nor did it know enough about pulp; it lacked both technological and marketing expertise.

Noranda Forest had seen this movie before. Tasmania may be halfway around the world, but North Broken Hill was facing a similar situation to what we'd encountered in British Columbia in the 1960s. A prime resource was going to waste — or, more accurately, to Japan. We were confident that our experiences could be transposed across the seas. We hadn't embarked on a forest-products project of this magnitude on foreign shores before (and haven't since — once bitten, twice shy), but pulp is a global commodity; as long as it gets aboard a ship headed in the right direction, distance means little. We knew that we could market our share of Wesley Vale's production as far away as Holland. The North Broken Hill–Noranda Forest fit seemed right from any standpoint.

In early 1988 Noranda Forest signed a joint-venture agreement to construct a $1-billion state-of-the-art mill with an annual capacity of 440,000 tonnes of bleached pulp, 300,000 of which would be slated for export. Our half interest in the project totalled $450-million — $200-million in equity over the two-year construction period, with the remainder financed through debt. We believed that the mill could be up and running in July 1991. Of course, Napoleon believed that it would be an easy march to Moscow.

At the time, however, all the players were enthusiastic and on-side. During the early stages of our negotiations, I'd been to both Australia and Tasmania. I toured North Broken Hill's existing plants, visited their offices in Melbourne and their bankers in Sydney, met with Premier Gray, and touched base with several state and federal ministers. Noranda Forest was warmly received by everyone, because the project had everything going for it. Wesley Vale would be the largest single industrial investment in Australian history — the third-largest (and, we hoped, the best) of over 250 such mills worldwide. It would comply with organic-chlorine-emission standards that were vastly more stringent than those in place elsewhere, thanks to a newly developed process involving pressurized oxygen. This meant that Wesley Vale would use only one-sixth the chlorine of any other kraft-process mill.

To substantiate these claims, we commissioned a comprehensive environmental-impact study, which was endorsed in writing by Peter Hodgman, Tasmania's minister of the environment. Meanwhile, an economic-impact study conducted by the University of Melbourne confirmed that Wesley Vale would create more than two thousand direct and indirect jobs during the construction phase. Once completed, it would provide seven hundred full-time operating jobs, labour productivity was projected as five times the national average, and Australia's balance of payments would improve to the tune of $1.4-billion throughout the 1990s. Robert Hawke, the Australian prime minister, announced a $300-million assistance package to help pay for the necessary infrastructure, allow equipment to enter the country duty-free, and permit its accelerated depreciation. Robin Gray, for his part, termed the project "an economic watershed." Instead, it very quickly proved to be economic quicksand.

Gray is a big, outdoorsy-looking man, not in the least flamboyant, but strong-willed and purposeful. His extremely low and rasping voice had caused the press to dub him "the Whispering Bulldozer." He led Tasmania's Liberal Party, which was in fact remarkably conservative — pro-development, pro-business, and a friend to industry, though capable of turning the screws when it suited their own purposes. But now, with state elections looming in May 1989, the party's traditional stance began to shift. Darcy Johnson, a senior adviser in Gray's office, convinced Gray that a growing political threat was posed by the Green Movement and other antidevelopment forces. So it was that environment minister Peter Hodgman drew up a list of eighty-five questions and concerns about the Wesley Vale project that went well beyond the issues addressed by our original impact statement.

I believe that Gray, bearing in mind his success at wringing price concessions out of North Broken Hill, was convinced that the impact statement was itself a bargaining ploy. Possibly he felt that he could swing votes his way by appearing to give the foreign interlopers — that is, Noranda Forest — a hard time. In any case, his cabinet devised a fresh set of environmental guidelines, which were presented to us in January 1989, a scant two hours before they were released to the media.

Gray announced that these new requirements were pioneering, pathfinding, and non-negotiable. Instead, they were deeply flawed. They failed to make a fundamental distinction between the mill's designed capacity and its probable operating performance. For example, the guidelines stipulated that odour emissions had to be maintained at extremely low levels, beyond which stiff fines would be imposed. Noise levels could not exceed forty-five decibels; otherwise the mill would have to cease operations for up to four hours. Last, the government expressed its dissatisfaction with the 99.9 percent protection afforded by secondary treatment of liquid effluent. Instead, it demanded a tertiary-treatment plant (at an additional cost of $24-million) that might or might not render the water that would be discharged two and a half kilometres offshore absolutely toxin-free and — at least in theory — safe to drink.

North Broken Hill and Noranda responded by terming the guidelines both scientifically inept and practically unachievable. No other facility in all the world had built a tertiary plant. Thus nobody knew what one was capable of doing, far less what it would cost; the $24-million price tag had been plucked out of thin air. We had already stated, in our environmental-impact study, that we would dilute the mill's liquid effluent by a factor of 150 to one. The proposed odour levels were half those that could be detected by the human nose. The proposed noise levels were already exceeded by other plants in the vicinity, and by planes landing and taking off at the airport in Burnie, the nearest town. And so on down the list. The guidelines simply could not be met, and we were faced with the prospect of killing the project before it killed us.

It wasn't long before Premier Gray began to have second thoughts, and by February 1989 he had changed his tune. He restated his support for Wesley Vale in even stronger terms, put distance between himself and Peter Hodgman, and warned against the activities of "narrow special-interest groups," perhaps in the belief that the Greens posed less of a political threat than he'd previously thought.

Gray did not, however, jettison the guidelines altogether. Instead, he said, the government would produce a document designed to "interpret" them, allowing, among other things, the release of organochlorines into Bass Strait. This was actually the least of anyone's worries. Most other pulp mills discharge their effluents into landlocked waters, which flush themselves very slowly, turning over every thirty years. But Bass Strait, because of its currents, entirely renews itself every six months. Coupled with the fact that Wesley Vale would use large amounts of oxygen and chlorine dioxide instead of chlorine per se, there was no practical or even conceivable likelihood that organochlorine compounds would accumulate off-shore — where there was, in any case, no commercial fishery.

Gray then announced that, in March, Parliament would vote on but not amend this interpretive document, because amendments would only cause further undue delays. Both Noranda Forest and North Broken Hill were ready to sign the document at once because the meter was running. We had to know exactly where we stood before we could proceed with the necessary equipment orders to get the project started.

Before the parliamentary vote we had to deal with Australia's Foreign Investment Review Board, located in Canberra. Based on his past experience, Robin Gray foresaw a bumpy ride. He predicted that "every antidevelopment group in the country will be beating a path to the prime minister's door; the federal cabinet is far less used to this kind of pressure than we are."

At this time the federal parliament was controlled by the Australian Labour Party, under Prime Minister Robert Hawke. Australia's constitutional division of powers meant that financial muscle was flexed primarily by the federal government; individual states did not control their own purse strings. The Labour regime, which was emphatically left-wing, had often taken a jaundiced view of Tasmanian development projects. Indeed, the federal minister for primary industries had been quoted as addressing Tasmania's forestry minister, Ray Groom, as follows: "Let me get this straight, Ray. First you want to log it all, then mine it, and then flood it." This attitude did not auger well for Wesley Vale.

Adverse commentary about the Noranda Forest–North Broken

Hill project now began to appear in the press. The thrust of the media's criticism was that there'd been an unseemly attempt to fast-track the project without sufficient debate.

Noranda had operated on the assumption that the executives of North Broken Hill were well acquainted with their own turf, that they knew how to stroke Australia's press and the politicians. Their methods of dealing with these two key players had seemed to us a bit rough-and-ready; nevertheless, we left matters largely in their hands. This was our undoing.

Our real blunder was a failure to grasp the peculiar dynamics of Australian politics — Liberal versus Labour, Hobart versus Canberra. The two levels of government were at daggers drawn, each looking for an excuse to score points at the other's expense. But we also failed to reckon with the unprecedented activities of the environmental movement, whose extremely effective campaign caught us woefully off guard.

The antimill forces were spearheaded by a group known as CROPS, which stood for Concerned Residents Opposing the Pulp Siting. Its leader was Christine Milne, a local schoolteacher who had been raised in Wesley Vale. She was tough and dedicated, but not open to a reasoned discussion. We offered to fly her to Canada so that she could see the Northwood complex for herself, but she refused, perhaps on the grounds that an expenses-paid junket would compromise her ideological purity. She declared, based on her group's "brief reading," that the Wesley Vale mill would both stink to high heaven and discharge organochlorines in harmful quantities — charges we could have effectively refuted. She also admitted that, despite her organization's name, the "siting" wasn't really at issue, because CROPS didn't want the project to go ahead anywhere in either Tasmania or Australia.

CROPS was supported in its efforts by environmentalists far and wide. Milne found a staunch ally in Bob Brown, a federal member of Parliament and Green activist, who made it his business to know the enemy at a glance. He stated darkly that "information about Noranda's record has come from other countries. Zimmerman has not just Australia against him, but the whole world. He has forgotten that people power changes what politicians do." Brown also intimated that Noranda had pressured the Tasmanian government to ease up on its environmental regulations because we feared the Canadian government would force us to play by the same rules both at home and abroad — that is, use Tasmania's guidelines as a benchmark so as to impose the same stringencies on our operations in British Columbia.

This intriguing theory distorted a number of comments I'd made to the Australian press. Asked about environmental safeguards, I'd replied that the mill would meet or surpass the highest standards achievable worldwide. Thus, I said, the safety margin at Wesley Vale would be far greater than was necessary, even though Australia's regulations were not then as rigid as those in Canada.

CROPS was also allied with Greenpeace International, which prevailed upon the ubiquitous David Suzuki to enumerate the horrors of dioxins. As it happened, the Canadian Broadcasting Corporation had produced — but not televised in Canada — a film implying, among other things, that airborne emissions from British Columbia's pulp mills enveloped Vancouver in a perpetual noxious fog. This film was released to the Australian television network, which aired it with predictable results. I pulled out all the stops on that one. In a formal complaint to the CBC, I noted that for an agency of the Canadian government to wilfully take sides against a legitimate Canadian enterprise acting in a responsible manner overseas was a "cocktail for disaster." Too late — because Noranda had already been shaken and stirred.

Meanwhile, Christine Milne and Bob Brown had begun a lobbying effort designed to persuade Paul Keating, the federal treasurer, to halt the Wesley Vale mill. Brown attacked Robin Gray on the grounds that he, Gray, was going to allow dioxin, which he labelled "one of the deadliest single molecules known to science" to emerge from both the mill's effluent pipe and its chimney stack, contaminating Bass Strait and the surrounding croplands.

The charges and countercharges began to fly thick and fast. To support his claim, Brown cited the findings of two lawyers from the United States who, on the basis of a flying visit to Australia, had decided that dioxins from the as-yet-unbuilt mill would pose a threat of cancer and birth defects. They said that Sweden (which they incorrectly thought to be the world's largest pulp producer) was planning to eliminate entirely the discharge of dioxins from all its mills, and that the United States Environmental Protection Agency was about to follow suit.

These suggestions were discredited at once. The Canadian Council of Resource and Environment Ministers (CCREM) stated that only one human health effect had been conclusively linked to exposure to dioxin — a temporary, non-life-threatening skin condition known as chloracne. No such link had been found to any long-term effects, including cancer, coronary disease, or congenital defects. The American Medical Association's Council on Scientific Affairs echoed these findings. A leading Swedish authority advised that neither dioxins nor furans were likely to form in the Wesley Vale plant, and that Sweden was not about to eliminate the discharge of dioxins (although individual producers, notably Sodra, had elected to go totally chlorine-free). The EPA, when somebody bothered to check, replied that it, too, had no such plan in mind.

But these and other even-handed views had marginal impact on the debate, which had begun to look more and more like the latest instalment of a particularly acrimonious family feud. The federal government's position seemed to be that Tasmania was run by headstrong yokels who had to be taught the error of their ways. Graham Richardson, the federal environment minister, spent the better part of two months grandstanding at every opportunity and finally arrived at a solution that would allow Hawke's regime to have its cake (the mill) and eat it, too (by appeasing the project's opponents).

Richardson announced that the Foreign Investment Review Board would approve Wesley Vale only if Noranda and North Broken Hill agreed to baseline studies that would establish the present toxicity of Bass Strait, and to a permanent monitoring system that would keep tabs on oceanographic and atmospheric conditions. Both these conditions were fine with us — but Richardson's final stipulation was too much to bear. He demanded still more guidelines, "superior" to Tasmania's, that would take his department four to six weeks to finish. This was presented to us sight unseen, take it or leave it.

In other words, having already spent a total of $20-million, Noranda Forest and North Broken Hill were being asked to bind themselves to a gaggle of mystery guidelines that, if the preceding ones were any indication, would quite probably be even more unachievable. At the same time we were in the position of having to confirm or cancel a further $30-million in advance equipment orders within the next twenty-four hours. The total outlay could very well climb as high as $50-million in the next six weeks, if indeed the guidelines were forthcoming that quickly. We had no idea what other rabbits the Australian government might pull out of its hat. And so, on March 15, 1989, Noranda Forest pulled the plug on the whole venture. Our official press release noted that we withdrew more in sorrow than in anger — but plenty of people, myself included, were actually boiling mad.

Noranda Forest's costly misadventures in Tasmania were the result of the company's being caught in a complex struggle between the federal and state governments; substitute "provincial" for "state," and the scenario will have a familiar ring for Canadians. Australia's federal ministers attacked us personally and corporately with blatant untruths and scientific gobbledegook, reversing their positions at whim. Tasmanian politicians were tiresome and confusing, changing their minds every other week. Their outlook was narrow and provincial in the extreme. (Nor did Robin Gray's waffling do him any good at the polls. The Labour party doubled its showing in the May elections and wound up holding the balance of power. Eventually the Liberals went down to defeat.) But the negative impact of all of this internecine political wrangling could have been substantially neutralized if Noranda and North Broken Hill had succeeded in getting their side of the story out to the press and creating public support for a project that would have been of unquestionable economic benefit to the people of Tasmania and Australia.

For my part, I certainly regret Noranda's involvement with North Broken Hill. They were less experienced than we'd been led to believe — surprisingly so, given their previous successes. But we, in turn, had failed to mind the store, particularly when it came to the vital public-relations component, and had relied too much on North Broken Hill's readings of the situation. Hindsight is easy, but losing $12-million — Noranda's share when all the marbles were counted up and everybody went home — definitely teaches a hard lesson.

The environmental movement claimed a famous victory in its successful derailing of the Tasmanian pulp mill, and attempted to springboard from it into further confrontations in other countries. But business operates on a global scale, too. Since Noranda's Tasmanian debacle, other companies have displayed reluctance to involve themselves in co-ventures Down Under. I was quoted at the time to the effect that the Australians couldn't run a corner store. I probably should not have said it, although I never hesitate to retell the story of their unreliability when asked.

As events transpired, Noranda could justifiably congratulate itself on a narrow escape at Wesley Vale. The mill would have come on-stream at the worst time imaginable in terms of the worldwide pulp market, lost huge amounts of money, and been very difficult to carry through the recession of the early 1990s. Later, of course, it would have made cash by the containerload.

In a lighthearted footnote I recall former Tasmanian premier Robin Gray's 1992 visit to Canada, when I hosted a dinner party in his honour. I told Gray I wasn't certain why I did so, because he'd cost my company $12-million and change.

"Adam," he responded ruefully, "I wonder why I'm attending your dinner party, because Wesley Vale cost me my government."

Interestingly, and as predicted to him, the same thing happened to Conrad Black with Fairfax in Australia, but at least he made money.

9

The Business
of the Board

Back in the early 1960s, before a number of directorships started coming my way, I asked Norman Urquhart what a board ought to do. Urquhart was a major player at the time, a senior member of Noranda's board, who'd been instrumental in financing a number of operations that became the Mining Corporation Group. His answer was short and to the point: "Support the management."

Urquhart's theory was that a board member is part of a team and should function rather like an auditor. He wasn't talking about blind loyalty or unreasoning acquiescence, which are a disservice to all concerned. Indeed, he was an advocate of hard questioning of management at every turn. If management's answers stood up under scrutiny, then the company's executives would be deemed to merit his and his fellow board members' approval.

But those, I note with a mixture of satisfaction and regret, were simpler days. Business was more straightforward and less burdened with a plethora of rules and government regulations. A code of honour prevailed among directors, even though it proved flexible on occasion: witness the director of my acquaintance (who shall remain unnamed) who engaged in stock trading immediately following a board meeting. Steeped in the brand of fiduciary puritanism that had been inculcated in me by Clarkson Gordon, I was duly shaken. I'd been taught that if ever you became party to privileged information, you promptly did nothing at all and forgot about it as soon as humanly possible. The offending director's rule was somewhat more elastic: "If you know about it, act on it." I decided that I much preferred Urquhart's and Clarkson Gordon's codes of conduct, and stuck to them unfailingly. I also bore in mind a third worthy admonition. "Don't do anything you wouldn't want to see on the front page of the newspaper."

Today's corporations are much larger and more diverse than those of thirty years ago. New forms of corporate ownership and ever more complicated accounting practices have given rise to all sorts of convenient rationalizations a company may use. New points of corporate vulnerability have emerged, along with new methods of fudging the issues and obscuring the facts. New rules and regulations are present in abundance, designed to curb allegedly new excesses, for example, those laws that seek to curtail insider trading and compel the revelation of significant shareholdings. Salaries and remuneration are today matters of public record. All these measures and more have been lumped under the rubric of "corporate governance." Fiscal savants and regulatory bodies, appalled (and one suspects baffled) by a wide range of egregious behaviour, have attempted to shed light on any number of sensitive areas that are open to abuse in an age of galloping takeovers, byzantine takeover defences, spectacular corporate failures, and salaries that would shame even a roomful of professional athletes.

Corporate governance is little more than a codification of what might just as well be termed common sense, honesty, and fair play. It relates to the individual morality, experience, and ambitions of each person involved. That's the drawback. At worst, it attempts to legislate human nature, and such attempts have not borne fruit in the past. Duplicity and greed are as old as humankind. Only the most naive would imagine that business would be universally conducted so as to achieve the greatest good for the greatest number were there no rules at hand. A cave-dwelling entrepreneur, having invented the first flint tool, quite probably bent his rudimentary mind to market share and cost competitiveness. The school-yard bully seeks to impose his will on weaker classmates, unobserved by the teachers or others who are bigger and stronger than he. Boardroom bullies will always be with us, lurking behind the veil of corporate privacy, pleading the need to preserve commercial intelligence and calm the fears of jumpy investors. Sadly the bullies are often among the best-recognized figures in the corporate world.

So it is that the rules keep on coming, framed to achieve entirely laudable aims. For example, the Toronto Stock Exchange has adopted a bylaw that requires a company to disclose its corporate-governance practices. A decent-enough concept, but experience shows that reality lags behind the best intentions.

The idea is that every corporate board have a separate committee charged with specific and fully accountable responsibilities having to do with management's operations, its succession, and its remuneration. This committee should also evaluate the performance of individual directors and of management as a whole. The TSE bylaw defines a board's broader mandate as overall stewardship responsibility. This includes the adoption of a strategic-planning process, the identification of principal risks and the measures that will be taken to contain them, the implementation of a communications policy, and the maintenance of the integrity of a firm's internal control and management-information systems. The board itself is to include a majority of individuals who qualify as unrelated directors. New nominees are to be presented to the full board; each member must participate in an orientation-and-education program and accept assignment to at least one committee. Compensation is to be set at a realistic level, and every board should ensure that it can function independently of management, defining the limits of management's responsibilities and developing objectives for which the CEO is held personally responsible. And so on, in even lengthier and more optimistic terms.

One must applaud any initiative that will enable corporations to better fulfil their purpose as trustees of other people's money. The TSE's guidelines are all well-intentioned and could work among like-minded individuals, but experience suggests that, were the guidelines adopted chapter and verse, performance would be all over the lot and, in the final analysis, not much different than it had been before.

Without question, there are certain responsibilities a board can clearly fulfil, among them choosing the CEO, nominating independent directors, and appointing the auditors. These are simple and straightforward mandates, but once the rules move beyond them, the fact is that a board can only do (and be held accountable for) so much when faced with headstrong management or recalcitrant ownership.

If board members are to be liable for the actions or inactions of management and owners, a potentially ruinous scenario, it's my belief that the indirect responsibilities identified by the TSE should either be plainly categorized as such or taken out of the board's hands altogether and performed by board members—but only in an advisory role.

How many layers of responsibility is it necessary and constructive for a corporation to have? Directors aren't management, and in my view they should play no direct part in the management process, although in fulfilling their stewardship role they will make certain key appointments and ask for reports on various procedures. But to what end? For example, a board may wish to acquaint itself with the corporation's "strategic planning" — a much misused phrase that means different things to different people. It's probably what I'd call operations planning: how and in what volumes business will be done in the coming year. Questions regarding labour, financing, acquisitions, and divestitures will also arise in the process, as is evident in any retrospective review of annual plans.

If this is so, what does or can an individual director's surveillance mean to strategic planning? That it happens at all? That there's general participation in the process? That the underlying assumptions are valid? That the external environment is properly assessed? Board members can ask all the questions they want — indeed, offer opinions till they're blue in the face — but with absolutely no assurance that their queries will be answered correctly by management or their concerns acted upon. Which is fine for advisers, but not so hot for a director if he or she is going to be held to any extent liable for what subsequently occurs.

Another reason the TSE's guidelines are likely to remain filed under "good intentions" is that, now as always, boards are composed of people. Each is a creature of his or her experience. That experience will be, to some extent, shared; everyone will have enjoyed some degree of success and recognition in the business world and is unlikely to be in the flower of youth. Beyond that common ground, personalities, motives, and inevitable foibles come into play. Some board members will do their homework; others will not. Some will speak up; others will be silent as the grave. As individuals, each is unique and uniquely valuable. As a group, they are vulnerable to domination by another individual or individuals, acting in accordance with their own designs. In a perfect world, as postulated by the TSE, your typical board meeting would be a case of all for one and one for all, with everybody bringing their particular talents to bear for the good of the enterprise involved. In the real world events unfold according to where the power lies. In the case of an inexperienced or factionalized board it may reside in the hands of a very few who think alike or who serve as mouthpieces for owners who've already made up their minds.

A great deal of nonsense is put forward about boards, and I want to dispel some popular misconceptions. I've had the privilege of serving on more than forty boards. (Some of these, although they were separate and operated separately, were actually outgrowths of Noranda.) Most were public companies, or companies in which other shareholders held at least a significant interest. On reflection, I've concluded that these companies divided four ways: some dealt in the production and distribution of tangible goods, while others were concerned with paper transactions; some had a controlling or dominant shareholder, while others did not. Noranda, as I've described, operated for many years as an independent producer of materials, but ultimately became dominated by Brascan, whose main raison d'être was financial wizardry. To Brascan, Noranda represented nothing more than one block of a gigantic pyramid. The dictates received in its latter-day boardroom were scarcely the result of a democratic process by which the shareholder or his agents sought and obtained a series of approvals, company by company and layer by layer. The guys who controlled the votes, whether or not they did so by virtue of some orderly process, ruled the day.

Which is the way of the world. A dominant owner will of course be represented on a company's board. This is right and proper. If one group or company buys a controlling interest in another, it's entitled to exercise all the control it wishes. It may very well steer the second company toward actions that would not take place if that firm were truly independent, but it's not, so there's no point in arguing. This tension is increasingly the case in Canada today and results in a two-tiered board: an A Team, comprising the owner's forces, and a B Team, comprising the remnants of the acquiree's directors and perhaps a couple of the supposedly nonaligned. In the latter case, make no mistake, an individual board member wields no power of any kind except logic and moral suasion, and can do little or nothing to shape the course of events. Indeed, I've come to the conclusion that, for such a company, the very existence of a board comes close to window dressing. The idea that minority rights will somehow be protected by a board's or a solitary member's intervention is naive. Possible, but not likely. In such a case minority shareholders are probably along for the ride. They may technically have legal rights, but the controlling interest will run the business exactly as it pleases. The minority's only protection is that, in the event of dividends, corporate reorganizations, or dispositions, they'll get the same deal as every other shareholder.

The directors of a controlled corporation may be, and at times are, useful in an advisory capacity, but they are far removed from the real decision-making. This takes place higher up the pyramid — perhaps when the person at its apex gets up in the morning and, while in the shower, figures out what's going to happen. This situation, I repeat, isn't in the least sinister; nor is it necessarily all that much worse than any other scenario. Many individuals who exercise personal control make excellent decisions. I'd favour a more democratic process every time, but owners rule their roosts by virtue of their having a bigger piece of the pie, period. It's probably ridiculous, other than to satisfy legal technicalities, for a company that's more than fifty-percent owned to bother with a board in the conventional sense. Once you're past the halfway point, an owner can and quite likely will do whatever suits its larger corporate (or any other) purpose.

Nevertheless, having been exposed to most of the permutations and combinations of boards over these past three decades, in terms of both operations and recruitment, I have reflected on what makes them good, bad, or indifferent.

There's no such thing as an ideal board member, even though some would argue (and waste time beating the bushes) for an all-purpose, touch-all-the-bases template — the corporate expression of political correctness. There are plenty of good people out there, but the search is somewhat narrowed from the start. For one thing, a suitable candidate is apt to be known to the existing board or have some association with someone in a management position within the company. The same person is apt to be the head of something. Rarely does a total stranger appear from nowhere. Rather, you aim to achieve a degree of camaraderie, which suggests that you go with someone you already know, like, and respect.

Once signed on, a new member is expected to do his or her homework. That doesn't mean an intimate acquaintance with all the minutiae of a given business. A grasp of the big picture, the environment in which the company operates, is an absolute must. Board members don't have to sit there poring over the fine print, because it's not their job to run the company. Unfortunately too many companies are entranced by the information explosion. The tendency is to present board members with every shred of material from every source, simply because it exists and can be so easily accessed, reproduced, and disseminated. Even the best-intentioned managers convince themselves that simply because they blitz the board with tons of material, the information therein is cogent, applicable, and easily absorbed. Not true.

The next criterion is that a board member be equipped for independent thought. You don't want a roomful of people sitting there nodding like perpetual-motion ducks. Members should think for themselves and speak up. The chairman should of course encourage this by directing traffic, maintaining focus, and giving everyone a chance to contribute. I've seen boards forced by their chairmen to foregone conclusions. On the other hand a good chairman knows how to get the right answers — perhaps the ones he wants to hear, but ideally ones the board as a whole has arrived at and come to want themselves. Indeed, every chairman or CEO should welcome a rigorous debate that puts prior judgments and knowledge to the test.

But even in the most open forum, debate must end at some point. In effect, a board must play devil's advocate, attempting to shoot down management's positions if there are demonstrable holes and supporting them if they are demonstrably sound.

Properly briefed and having formulated positions of their own, members will no doubt voice any number of questions. It's the duty of management to respond; they've got to do their homework, too. Members should not only seek clarification of specific points, but ought to leave the meeting unburdened by lingering doubts and satisfied as to the course of action that will be pursued. (This, too, has its pitfalls. I am a great believer in consensus, arrived at after full and frank discussion, but I realize that a natural human tendency, once the majority position has been arrived at, is to close ranks.) It can happen, however, that a member cannot support the group's conclusion. If so, that member should accept the decision as gracefully as possible — but if doubts remain on a contentious point, should write to the chief executive, explaining the reasons behind his or her continued dissent. That might be dismissed as covering one's ass, but it's right and proper to go on the record in this way if circumstances warrant.

Looking back on my directorial experiences, I think that the best, in an operating sense, took place on the boards of foreign companies. The first, Royal Dutch Paper Mills, had a very small board — five Dutch, two Canadians, and one Austrian. The company had achieved remarkable growth by means of a combination of mergers, acquisitions, and construction. When I was a director its board was governed by clearly defined protocol. The materials provided to us were broad-based yet concise, a typical agenda was confined to major issues, and management were presented to us in a formal way at every meeting. Everyone was extremely well prepared, and hard decisions were usually reached after stringent examination. In all, this was the sort of board directors dream about. Even though there was a dominant shareholder present (MacMillan Bloedel, which I represented along with one other person), its interests were never seriously at odds with those of the other shareholders. Thus, we were never perceived as a serious impediment. In every particular, the Royal Dutch experience embodied what the TSE bylaw is currently striving to achieve.

This is also the case with the Pittston Company, an entirely independent American company with an eleven-person board who were largely unknown to one another prior to their election. This board operates much along the lines of Royal Dutch, but with less formality. The board usually gets together for dinner the night before a meeting. There may be one or two committee meetings earlier that day or before a full-scale meeting the next. Pittston takes pains to educate its members, making sure we visit various sites and get to know the operating personnel. No one is burdened with inconsequential detail; the main thrust of every operation is clearly understood. Meetings are limited to consideration of major items and to absorbing and evaluating the committees' reports. Again, no one feels dominated by any individual or group, and a truly constructive consensus emerges, in which everyone plays a part.

The Toronto Dominion Bank is a huge entity whose board is of necessity rather ponderous. Like the proverbial supertanker, a bank takes a while to turn around; nevertheless, it can and does happen. The TD's management is reasonably attentive to questions from the board, but it would be difficult if not impossible to divert them from their chosen course of action. A bank, almost by definition, is compelled to make major decisions independent from the board — the definitive example of its members acting in an advisory capacity much of the time. Individual directors must therefore be at ease with the company's procedures and with the people who are implementing them within myriad operations. However, no current director of the TD has ever to my knowledge, felt that his or her voice was not both heard and listened to.

Finally I think of five more companies, all of which had controlling shareholders — three British, one American, and one Canadian. These were Steetly, Maple Leaf Foods, Celanese Canada, Royal Insurance, and Noranda. In every case, the ownership had, and amply demonstrated, an agenda of its own. It was perfectly overt and certainly not subject to serious alteration or amendment by the so-called independent directors — but I'm not certain that any of the firms is any the worse for this. All five are still more or less thriving, arguably little better or worse off than they would have been had they been controlled by independent directors.

Celanese, however, distinguished itself in an extraordinary way. It was a sixty-percent-owned subsidiary of an American company — a highly technical business whose management and ownership directors knew far more about it than anyone else did. I realized that I was on the wrong board when the U.S. representatives showed up one day, announced that they'd recruited two new Canadian directors, and added that one of these people had been appointed chairman. Actually they'd made a good choice, which proved they didn't need me around to help them.

Noranda's board, when I first began to attend its meetings, was quite old-fashioned, heavy on management reports but short on presentations outlining future activities, which were deemed to be the province of the management. After the Brascan acquisition of course, Noranda's board became a mere cipher.

MacMillan Bloedel, at the time Noranda gained controlling interest, had a very legalistic board, having been run for years by Jack Clyne, followed by Cal Knudsen, both lawyers. It was rigid and bureaucratic, and provided members with reams of material in which the woods were obsured by impenetrable stretches of trees. When I and four other Noranda representatives joined, we broadened the horizons. The company no longer has a major shareholder, and the board's operations have changed.

I think also of Confederation Life, whose collapse in August 1994 has entered history as a disaster of major proportions. I've been asked: why didn't its directors do something to avert the calamity? This question is impossible to answer fully, for legal reasons, but I can assert that the board gave it their best shot for two long years before throwing in the towel. They maybe didn't act as quickly as hindsight now suggests, but they certainly made a vigorous attempt. In fact a case could be made that they behaved in textbook fashion in the policyholders' interest. The company had done business for 125 years in a staid and perhaps unimaginative way. It was Canada's third-largest insurance firm, and its downfall was almost unthinkable. It had always been heavily invested in real estate, with positive results; no one could have foreseen that real estate would go off the cliff as it did. As the extent and duration of the crash began to sink in, the board took every measure at its disposal. It moved to a wholesale change in management and enlisted the aid of every imaginable relevant outside adviser. During the final six months everyone was convinced that the board was working on a viable rescue plan, which involved Great West Life. When Great West exited abruptly, our efforts came to naught, with results that are a matter of record. The lesson learned from the Confed crash is this: the task of marshalling resources to assess a problem and initiate a remedy is not as simple as some believe. No one, particularly a common shareholder, should be misled into thinking that a company's directors can necessarily save them from disaster.

In addition to the directorships I've held in commercial corporations, I've also been blessed by membership on the boards of several nonprofit institutions, including a neighbourhood community centre, the United Appeal, a major hospital, a handful of private schools, amateur athletic organizations, universities, consultation organizations, and a concert hall.

The boards of all these enterprises work for free, in an egalitarian, noncompetitive environment. Usually they are an eclectic mixture of men and women, which makes for a highly stimulating discussion. The business-trained person is often in the minority. Members range in their thinking from believing their role to be purely advisory to expecting to be fully in charge.

Nonprofit boards tend to assess their problems in a truly open fashion. The coalescence of the views that is usually distilled from their deliberations supports the continuance of worthy institutions with limited means of support. The noncombative, collegial attitude among nonprofit directors results in a productive, purposeful board — a model that should be more widespread in corporate boardrooms.

The bottom line of corporate governance concerns the use or misuse of wealth. A corporation is entrusted with other people's money in the form of bonds and stock. Investors are attracted because they believe that the business can provide them with a satisfactory return within the shelter of limited liability. As a business grows, so does its complexity, to the point that the people at the top know more and more about less and less, while those engaged in day-to-day operations fully grasp just the details of their own small corner. The only way to get a handle on this complexity is by a process that transmits information efficiently and accurately from the shop floor to the boardroom and vice versa.

The choice of able employees must be the top priority of senior management, just as the CEO's appointment is the prime responsibility of the board. There are three possible models of CEO selection: unilateral appointment, developed consensus, and organized search. In my experience the CEO of a controlled company is very often chosen by the owner and presented to the board on a platter. The owner wants a loyalist, his own person in place. This is not necessarily a negative way to go. Its obvious drawback is that it fails to consider other candidates.

The second practice is a variant of the first. Over time, one or two people gradually emerge as likely and capable heirs to the top job. This can either lead to an orderly and seamless transition, or it can perpetuate faulty policies/operations, stultify thinking, and fan the flames of head-office politics.

The third method, and to my view, the best, is a full-scale open search. Present employees should be welcome to apply, and if the best candidate emerges from them, he or she should certainly get the nod. In the process, however, the search committee gets to review a range of fresh faces and new ideas. This may yield surprising results. Some people imagine that the top jobs are all sewn up, that no one is prepared to jump ship or seek new pastures. But that's not the case. When I was put in charge of finding a new chief executive for Confederation Life, the company's prospects weren't entirely sunny. Rather than scaring applicants off, this aroused a sense of challenge, and we could have hired almost anybody we wanted (barring the bank chairmen, who tend to stick close to home). In the end, if an internal candidate wins out over the competition, he or she is fortified by the knowledge that he or she has beaten the best the free market has to offer.

The next component of corporate governance is board and executive remuneration. I don't believe Canadian directors are overpaid, but an increasing number of executives are. Now that these figures are matters of public record, there seems to be a contest over which CEO earns the biggest bucks. I've often heard the questionable rationale "If we don't pay X so-and-so, we'll lose him." Not necessarily, and even if it were true, so what? Any significant top-level job will attract a host of excellent candidates at sensible salary levels. Every CEO at a big bank now commands in excess of a million dollars annually. If such a post became vacant and the pay was limited to half that sum, there is no question that many suitable replacements would come forward — some of them from within the institution itself.

There was a time when a CEO might have had to struggle by with ten or twelve times the salary of the company's lowest-paid wage earners — $100,000 and $10,000 respectively. Another factor that kept the lid on the cash drawer was the so-called "step value" of a given corporate post. Thus, if a vice-president received $70,000, a president was content with $105,000, and so on up and down the line. This carefully structured salary scheme went out the window when union contracts jacked up the base level. At the top, a strange and wonderful assortment of bonuses and stock-option plans, many of them unrelated to individual performance, became the order of the day.

Business has to some extent invited increasing scrutiny of its activities, but much of the behaviour corporate governance is designed to contain is stimulated by externally generated demands. The professional investing community has institutionalized greed by worshipping quarterly (even monthly) results. The tax laws have created under-the-table manoeuvrings, because they're viewed in some quarters as little more than forced confiscation of honestly gotten gains. When taxes approach the fifty-percent mark, people begin to think they'll share no more and batten down to look out for Number One.

The rules of disclosure, as outlined in the TSE bylaw, cannot eliminate corporate malfeasance. In some failures there is a deliberate attempt to falsely gain investor confidence, if not to deceive outright. The techniques employed, if not disinformation per se, boil down to the issuing of impossibly complicated data that only the most sophisticated analyst could hope to grasp.

The TSE's guidelines are hardly less complicated, and they are bound to be welcomed by the nation's lawyers, who can look forward to a new source of income interpreting them for the rest of us. Another culprit when it comes to opaque fiscal utterance is the Institute of Chartered Accountants, which perpetuates the false notion that accountancy is a complicated science impenetrable to the uninitiated. Disclosure does no earthly good if ordinary mortals can't figure out what's being disclosed.

Nor is disclosure improved by indulging in crystal-gazing. One school of thought holds that companies should articulate their future plans and be held to them. Experience suggests that in many businesses, including the resource industries, this is possible only to a degree. A mining company, for example, may have more or less solid prospects, but its management never really knows when an important discovery may pan out and can't pledge with absolute certainty that it will meet performance expectations by a certain time. Nor should an investor demand this. Owning shares is in itself a speculation on the future, expressing the shareholder's conviction that a given company promises better returns than another, that its management is better equipped to take appropriate action when the need arises and circumstances warrant.

The onus is therefore on the investor, and caveat emptor should still be the motto, even in an era of class-action suits. Regrettably lawyers have convinced the courts and the regulatory bodies that society should be protected from itself. If this attitude is to prevail, I believe that the penalties ought to be limited to some reasonable amount, say, the original investment, compounded at a realistic interest rate over the period of duress.

And who, by the way, is actually being protected by all these over-reaching rules and regulations? Obviously it's the shareholders, but who are they in this day and age? The majority of corporate share-holders are either other corporations (which ought to know what they're getting into) or funds (ditto) that consolidate the assets of numerous participants. Of course the fabled small investor should be given a fighting chance — and so he is, by the fund manager, who has (or should have) ample resources to make a considered profes-sional judgment of the companies in which the fund chooses to invest. Certainly all the advertisements one sees around each RRSP deadline make this very claim.

The other side of the disclosure coin is worth a moment's thought. I repeat: who is the shareholder? Often the corporation itself doesn't know who owns it. Sizeable blocks of shares are often held in the names of bank and trust nominees, numbered companies, and so forth. I don't necessarily ascribe some nefarious purpose to these sub-terfuges, but one wonders why they're necessary or desirable. And if there's an element of skulduggery involved, why should these investors expect to be cut any slack if things go awry? It would be a good thing if companies knew who actually, beneficially, owned their shares. The only possible negative is that, if the shareholders were indeed plotting a takeover, they'd be effectively smoked out. But a corporation's top executives and directors are entitled to know who owns it, who wishes to own more of it, and who may be thinking of assuming control. Indeed, there are probably just as many companies who would like to have major shareholders as there are those to whom the prospect is anathema.

It is a truism that business must operate with the consent of society and be subject to the laws of the land. By all means let's ensure that society — and particularly investors — know the knowable and understand the basic financial data that will enable them to grant informed consent. As long as the concept of corporate governance serves these ends, it's all to the good. When it attempts to achieve the impossible — to remove all risk and remedy every human failing — it too will fail, both in the nation's boardrooms and in the minds of ordinary citizens.

AT THIS POINT IT MIGHT BE WORTH mentioning a few home truths that always emerged in connection with boards:

1. Every business forecast that goes beyond one year will inevitably show growth or ascension or up-tick or whatever you want to call it. Mankind is chronically, perhaps genetically, incapable of predicting a decline. The corollary of this is that things never happen as predicted.

2. Further on the above, every company's hurdle rate is about fifteen percent, and every request for capital expenditure will come in showing a rate of return within ten percent of fifteen percent — that is, it will be between 13.5 percent and 16.5 percent, put usually only tenths of a percent off fifteen.

3. When you want to know what's really going on in a business, ask the shipper. The shipper undoubtedly knows the most

about any business that makes things — and has no idea of the relevance of his information.

4. Those who advocate or advertise some percentage annual compound growth rate as their performance goal are propounding a mathematical impossibility. No one has ever made it or ever will, because the workings of compound interest would bring the total to something like owning the world in thirty years.

10

The Business of Government

Over the years, I've been dismayed to see business often being merely a bystander in the formation of public policy about business matters. Business and government, as much as French- and English-speakers, could be described as the country's two solitudes. This dichotomy isn't entirely surprising; in many ways the two mind-sets are at odds, and good businesspeople seldom make good politicians. The body politic is seldom enriched by their presence, and of those who've tried to make the transition few have fared well.

Businesspeople are frequently aghast at the other-worldly theorizing and feckless tinkering in which many politicians are prone to indulge. In return I suspect that our governors believe their duty is to keep the world safe from the depredations of business, and that to work hand in hand would be against the public interest. Most legislators and regulators wouldn't dream of approaching a given industry, which surely knows (or ought to know) the most about its own strengths and shortcomings, and saying, "How can we help you?"

The problem is that governments are suspicious of the business community. They've been burned in the past by handing out money and concessions to corporate snake-oil salesmen and fly-by-nighters. Because the distance between those in public office and those in the corner office tends to be so great, politicians have few reliable sources of information when they need objective advice about a particular industry or company.

Yes, business makes almost ceaseless representations to every level of government. We hold joint meetings by the score, frequently to scant effect. There are one-shot responses, bright ideas that surface, enjoy their brief hour in the sun, then sink from view. Prosperity Initiatives, Third Options, and well-publicized trade junkets come and go, having provided little more than an exotic photo opportunity for perambulating politicians and their entourages.

Stop the average voter on the street, and you will find that he or she believes that business has a hotline to Ottawa, that moguls and mandarins confer hourly to shape the course of history while feathering their own nests. This is purest fiction: witness the fact that the government is frequently driven by large-scale industry or corporate failures to create ad hoc commissions, stopgap studies, and every kind of consultation short of Ouija boards. That's not constructive dialogue; it's crisis management.

Even in the current climate of massive cutbacks, Canadians still accept government intervention and support as a way of life. Despite their protestations to the contrary, they expect the rulers of the day to leap in and *do* something — and they all too often comply, much to business's constant dismay.

The trouble is that voters often buy a pig in a political poke. The electorate thrashes to and fro, voting for the most part negatively — *against* a detested or mistrusted incumbent regime, not *for* the policies of its opponents. If these latter are articulated in any detail, they're apt to be dismissed once the results are in as "only campaign promises." The supposition is that everything said during the heat of an election is largely if not purely for effect, and that the speaker shouldn't be held accountable. (One harks back to Kim Campbell's blurted assertion that campaigns were not a useful forum for the intelligent debate of policy issues!) It comes as a rude surprise whenever a party actually follows through on its rhetoric, and this sticking to a preelection agenda virtually guarantees that it will be defeated four years down the line. But throwing the rascals out, at first glance an attractive prospect, only ensures that fresh rascals are voted in, as evidenced by the odd events in Ontario, where the past three provincial elections have produced three widely differing majority governments — Liberals, then New Democrats, then Tories. Indeed, all across the land, we see a mad rush to the opposite political pole on the theory (proved wrong with dreary regularity) that the alternative can't be all that much worse than its predecessor. Incumbent politicians everywhere shiver in their boots, and with good reason. It's always "time for a change," but nothing important really ever changes. Perhaps, just perhaps, this turmoil persists because the present economic order does not truly serve the people. The elite come out on top as usual, but the vast majority remain frustrated and dissatisfied.

It's safe to say that no politician is interested in thinking more than two years ahead. Halfway through a government's mandate, reelection becomes the sole priority. This is the genesis of any number of quite remarkable flip-flops and upendings. Remember the Trudeau-era Liberals on wage and price controls, Mulroney's Tories on free trade, the latter-day Grits on the GST. The usual excuse, trotted out like clockwork, is that the previous office-holders have left the city's, province's, or country's affairs in such dire straits that all bets are off, and everything pledged with hand on heart during the heat of the campaign is shelved for future study or postponed till better days. Not surprisingly ordinary citizens become cynical about the whole process and adopt the view espoused by the bumper-sticker slogan Don't Vote, It Only Encourages Them.

But vote we must, so let's turn our attention instead to the manner in which our governments practise their various interventions into the economy.

Take, for example, job creation. Everyone wants and needs a job. As a result, job creation is at the top of any government's priority list, even though how best to go about it is open to debate. Business would prefer that politicians and bureaucrats get their own affairs in order, thereby creating a climate or framework that's conducive to private enterprise, which will then carry the ball. Business will respond to favourable conditions, the market will allocate capital, viable firms will thrive and take on workers, and the losers will fall by the wayside. Governments should by all means stand watch over the private sector to see that it behaves lawfully and serves the public interest. And so they do, which is why businesses both big and small are awash in rules and regulations that safeguard the environment, ensure fair competition, protect employees and consumers, and encourage business activity where it might not otherwise be attractive to private interests. It seems to me, however, that the promises or slogans common to every political party — providing jobs and getting the economy moving — have all too often produced significant distortions in the national economy and encouraged or institutionalized regional selfishness. Funds may be limited nowadays, but this sort of thing will come back to haunt us as the provinces, in the wake of the 1995 Quebec referendum results, demand and almost certainly receive enhanced powers of every kind.

Far too many provincial job-creation programs, assisted by federal supplements and subsidies, have not resulted in significant gains in long-term profitable employment. The grants lavished on fast-talking promoters who pledge to resuscitate plants that ought to be mothballed or bulldozed are matters of record in the resource field. Most of these schemes were simply flagrant pork-barrelling. I think particularly of the Port Cartier pulp mill, located in former prime minister Brian Mulroney's home riding of Manicouagan, Quebec, and of the Cyprus Anvil mine, up in Yukon, the home riding of his deputy prime minister, Erik Nielson. Neither was an economically viable project; neither had a prayer of attracting private funds. Port Cartier was a boondoggle from the outset, and now is in the hands of its third or fourth owners. The original Anvil mine made money, but its reestablishment by means of a grant accelerated the decline of zinc prices in an already depressed market. Both these sites, along with many others, would have held no appeal for a prudent and legitimate operator who didn't expect to be paid with public monies to run them. That's not pump-priming; it's force-feeding.

Orchestrated redundancy is another peculiarly Canadian phenomenon. To cite just one example, all of the country's telephone wire could easily have been supplied by a single plant, yet there were individual production centres in virtually every province to guarantee that local purchases would support local interests. The same could be said for many other goods and services. This sort of unnecessary duplication leads to ridiculously expensive inefficiency and exacerbates the very problems it's designed to redress. A money-losing plant contributes nothing; on the contrary it usually requires even greater infusions of capital as the years roll on. The local workforce waits for the other shoe to drop, as it inevitably will. It may be deemed cruel to put people out of work, but what is the sense in maintaining an empty charade? Certain realities, although unpleasant, are inescapable.

For example, if there aren't any fish, then the Newfoundland outports are doomed. They may be close-knit communities with generations of living off the sea tying them to their villages, but without a fishery the inhabitants must turn to other ways of earning a living. All too often Canadian taxpayers have been asked to maintain and pay for economic life-support systems that, to put it bluntly, the citizens of other less affluent or profligate countries somehow manage to do without.

I have pondered long and hard about formulating a set of conditions that could improve cooperation both among the various
regions and between business and federal government. My proposal
is based on the premise that what business fears above all else are
sudden change and nonmarket intrusions into their affairs. It is also
based on the experiences recited in this book.

All competent businesspeople must accept risk, but if their businesses are being run so as to rise or fall on their own merits, to attract
capital and to turn a profit in accordance with the ebb and flow of
free market forces, the appearance of competitors armed with enormous modernization or resettlement grants is hard to swallow. These
beneficiaries of government largesse may enjoy capital costs that are
twenty percent below their competitors'. What can the legitimate
businessperson do to redress this unfairness? The temptation is to join
the lineup at the public trough. Otherwise, you're placing your company and its shareholders and workers at a permanent disadvantage.

Grants are unlikely to cease, but they ought to be earned, rather
than handed out holus bolus with precious few strings attached. The
Canadian Pulp and Paper Association advocates a system by which
grants would be administered through income-tax returns. Success
would precede benefits; a company would receive easements only if
it put in its own money up front, then made an operation work
before it reaped a reward. This isn't a particularly original idea by
any means. Indeed, it goes back to the 1930s, when the price of gold
was fixed at very low figures. As a result, gold mines were dropping
like flies, so the government instituted a three-year tax exemption,
which soon became the general rule for new mines of any description. This is how Gaspé Copper got its start. Unfortunately the
system eventually became prone to abuse and was shelved in the
aftermath of the 1967 Carter Commission on taxation, but while it
lasted, this system was attractive from several standpoints. In one
sense it didn't cost a penny, because the taxes were simply deferred.
The public may have forgiven some taxes, but there wasn't a direct,

out-of-pocket expenditure or a budgetary cost; the government served in essence as a promoter, not as an outright donor.

I have spoken of the difficulties endured by the forest industry not having an acceptable means of consulting with governments. That is but one example of a general Canadian problem.

During the free-trade negotiations, the federal government made a step in the right direction toward improved consultation by creating a central, largely private-sector group called the International Trade Advisory Committee, which oversaw the work of something like fifteen separate Sectoral Advisory Groups on International Trade (SAGITs). By their very nature, these groups were elite. Their members were chosen by some impenetrable bureaucratic or political numbers game to reflect a preconceived balance of the electorate. Participants were summoned on the basis of where they lived and whether they were known to the selectors as opposed to being invited by the industry sectors. Despite these shortcomings in the selection process, the SAGITs were a step in the right direction and were much better than nothing. Sadly they pretty well died on the vine when the free-trade deal was done, but I believe we should take the core of the idea and work toward the establishment of a group of permanent SAGITs or trade associations that would be organized by the industries concerned rather than by bureaucrats. Existing associations — for example, the Canadian Pulp and Paper Association, the Retail Council of Canada, and the Canadian Bankers Association — offer sound models of organization for these new entities.

Suppose that, for starters, we divide Canada's industries into twenty broad categories. Others may occur to you, but let's call them (in alphabetical order) Air and Sea Transport; Agriculture and Fishery; Automobile Manufacturing and Sales; Broadcast Media; Culture (the performing and visual arts); Chemicals and Plastics; Electrical Manufacturing; Financial Services; Food Processing; Forest Products; Franchises and Small Services; Heavy Manufacturing; Land Transport (railways and trucking); Minerals; Steel; Oil and Gas;

Printing and Publishing; Retailing; Textiles and Apparel; and Travel and Hospitality.

Ideally every company in the sector would belong to the association, which would be fully funded by the membership. The chief executive or chief operating officer of each member company would be an executive board member of the association. The association would have a full-time president and be fully and permanently staffed. The chairmanship would rotate annually, which would spread the workload (not to mention the praise and blame) around, cut down on political back-stabbing, and keep grumbling to a minimum. Most important, each association would maintain at its own expense an up-to-the-minute, comprehensive database on conditions and developments relevant to its members.

In my experience in the pulp-and-paper industry, the formation of such an association has led to a number of informed and well-considered position papers on matters affecting the industry, including taxation, trade, the environment, transportation, labour, and technology. Sometimes, of course, the membership becomes split into two or more camps, which the final document or recommendation duly notes in its exploration of the opposing points of view. If only a few members are at odds with the majority, they still have the chance to air a dissenting opinion.

The existence of a trade association removes from politicians and bureaucrats who deal with that industry the excuse of claiming that its executives haven't gone on record to present their viewpoints before a government policy is implemented. They would know in detail what the industry thinks because they would be getting constant feedback from the top people. They might choose to adopt some other course of action, but they'll have had the opportunity to consider the industry's best advice. The guiding principle is that no one knows more about what's happening in a given field than the people on the front lines.

The drawbacks to this approach are largely illusory. One is a predictable measure of scepticism among the public who may feel that business and government are getting too cosy. They may have visions of deals struck in back rooms, powerful interests at work behind the scenes, politicians in the thrall of cigar-smoking magnates, and so forth. My rejoinder is that governments are now so afraid of being caught in bed with business that they've gone out of their way to foster — indeed, have developed a vested interest in — perpetual fragmentation and lack of consultation. Turf protection is a factor here: a minister or his bureaucrats stake out and jealously defend their power base, failing to make use of their potential allies in industry. Surely the sensible thing would be for government to say to business: Look, we've got a problem. It concerns your industry. You know how to fix it, or at least you say you do, so go ahead and fix it.

Recent attempts to pitch the idea of SAGITs at the federal level took place during 1995, when a group of retired executives, of which I was one, met with Industry Minister John Manley, but the end result was a letter advising me that the department was opting instead for a consultative mechanism study, and I should stay tuned. Which I've done, with predictable results. I don't claim that SAGITs are a magic wand, but they could be up and running within a month and they wouldn't cost the taxpayers a dime. If nothing else, they'd succeed in getting the nation's industries talking to each other — a meaningful advance, because all too often we wind up boxed into our own small corners knowing precious little about the difficulties faced by firms in different fields, even though our problems are actually much the same. Information would go into a common pool and be accessible by all concerned. Perhaps a number of provincial subassociations would spin off from the national bodies, which would make life easier for the federal government in its dealings with the provinces. If everyone were looking at the same numbers, it would put the lid on hyperbole and emphasize the need for a consensus view. One might usefully speculate that some of the pitfalls of the softwood-lumber fiasco could have been avoided if such a body had been in place. At the very least the accumulated data would prove invaluable when it came to community-outreach programs and public education.

I'd like to see business organize itself so that its voice can be brought into the fact-finding and policy-making process in ways that are both proper and productive. I don't believe that business can or should participate actively in initiating legislation; that's where the line between the public interest and private interests should continue to be drawn. But business should play a more significant role in developing and administering regulations within the law, in fields such as the environment and health and safety.

11

Business and Government Dance the Dialectic

My first real contacts with Ottawa began when the Mining Association of Canada was up in arms over the recommendations put forward by the Carter Commission, which in its wisdom had decided that a buck was a buck and ought to be taxed everywhere at the same rate. This would have spelled disaster for the mining industry. The industry, led by John Bradfield of Noranda Mines, Jack Barrington of Falconbridge, and Ralph Parker of Inco, fought these proposals tooth and nail, with a degree of success.

I also recall a number of debates concerning the issue of copper pricing. Canadian copper fabricators had traditionally paid smelter operators a reduced price for copper destined for strictly Canadian use. Jake Warren, deputy minister of Trade and Commerce at the time, proposed that the fabricators be permitted to estimate how much they'd require for the coming year, then order it at the lower price. This gladdened the hearts of the fabricators, who saw an opportunity to requisition a vast quantity, run it through their mills, and ship it out the back door at world prices. The discussions with Warren and his minions provided me, in my role of assisting Alf Powis, with a crash course in mandarin relations.

Eventually I became more active in the mining association and served as chairman of its tax committee for several years. We made presentations whenever a federal or provincial budget rolled around, and spoke out against whatever we perceived as injustices whenever they arose. On balance we did fairly well, partly because the industry had enjoyed favourable treatment in the past, which had been seen to pay off in mutually beneficial ways.

The meetings between government and the Canadian Pulp and Paper Association, in which I began to participate early on, were marked by the able chairmanship of Bob Fowler of CPPA, an articulate and almost patrician individual who'd himself been an Ottawa mandarin. He was later succeeded by the quiet-spoken but smart and sensitive Howard Hart. Each year the association prepared a list of issues we presented to various government departments and followed up by means of further representations. Fowler insisted always that our briefs be well researched, and he made sure they were presented by board members who were both fully conversant with the issues and could speak to them in a cogent but seemingly unrehearsed way. He knew how to zero in on the areas of prime concern, to steer clear of rhetoric and exaggeration, and to focus on practical, attainable solutions. A lot of this went on in the committee rooms, but a fair amount took place behind the scenes as well. Fowler knew his way around Ottawa; he had ready access to the powers that be, functioning more or less as a one-man lobby. Somehow in the 1960s and 1970s these contacts seemed to be a more civilized form of discourse than they've since become, which I regret. As I've described, we resorted to lobbyists to present our case in Washington during the softwood-lumber dispute — out of necessity, because otherwise we'd never have opened the doors. That's too bad, but at least we were in the other guy's backyard. If you have to pay a third party to gain access to one of your own elected representatives, as seems now to have happened in Canada, then the "system" is debased.

I would argue that the ability of business to influence government is vastly overrated in the public mind. Some years ago I had dinner with Jack Munro, who then headed the International Woodworkers of America; he was a pretty good friend, although firmly ensconced on the opposite side of the bargaining table. He asked why I and the rest of the "eastern bastards" couldn't go to the banks and make them change their staggeringly high interest rates. His theory seemed to be that this could be accomplished by a few words in the right ears and the stroke of a pen — thus easing the pain of his members who were suffering, like most Canadians, under huge mortgage payments.

Munro's remedy was somewhat less than practical. Throughout the late 1980s and early 1990s, the heads of resource companies strove to impress on the powers that be the harmful effects of high interest rates and tight money policies on Canada's resource industries. Inflation was being stamped out, no question about it, but we were trapped underfoot. For five years resource firms made no money at all. Indeed, they lost colossal amounts, were unable to upgrade their plants or make needed capital investments, and this imperilled their longer-term competitive position. Times have improved, but not sufficiently to make up for half a decade of endless bad news.

In conjunction with Alf Powis and George Petty, head of Repap Enterprises Inc., I urged several modifications to the federal government's policy of the time. First was that it consider a currency devaluation, accompanied by a wage freeze and a tax exemption for newly won profits if these were invested directly in capital improvements within two years. This strategy had worked wonders for the Swedish and Finnish forest industries, but foundered when government expenditures got out of hand and inflation took hold once more. I also advocated a concerted attack on both the federal and the provincial deficits. I was alarmed by the fact that Ontario's deficit in 1991–92 was heading toward $8-billion, a figure that by now has taken on an almost nostalgic glow.

Over a period of several months in 1987 I corresponded with then governor of the Bank of Canada John Crow, the chairmen of the largest chartered banks, former prime minister Mulroney, and finance ministers Mike Wilson and Don Mazankowski. I acknowledged Crow's determined attempts to keep a lid on inflation and applauded his desire to maintain a stable currency, but argued that at eighty-seven cents U.S., he'd picked the wrong level to stabilize it at. Specifically my colleagues and I recommended the more realistic and to my mind more advantageous range of seventy-eight to eighty cents. Admittedly a devaluation of that magnitude would have to be carefully managed, but we pointed out that the dollar had risen by twenty percent during the preceding four years, and that what had gone up could and should go down by means of a series of declines in the exchange rate along the order of thirty-five basis points each. My arguments were fortified with papers from the C.D. Howe Institute, the speeches of Sweden's former minister of finance, Kjell-Olof Feldt, the writings of other academics and financial authorities, and all the charts and graphs I could lay my hands on.

Nowadays of course it's become accepted wisdom that a tight-money, high-rate policy went on too long and resulted in enormous damage, especially to Canada's exporters, but also to countless other businesses and individuals. At the time, however, anyone who opposed that policy was crying in the wilderness. I suspect that my letters were written off by their Ottawa recipients as the self-serving voice of what's usually termed a "special-interest group." But every corporate executive has the right and duty to speak out on behalf of the best interests of his or her company, and those interests are broader than is generally assumed. They include the well-being of shareholders and workforces — and by extension, or so I'd argue, the well-being of a given province or region; indeed, of the entire nation.

It could of course be argued that business doesn't know enough to make a meaningful contribution at the policy level. We don't have the latest unemployment figures at our fingertips; we don't know where the latest waves of immigration are coming from. We aren't aware of the implications that flow from, say, a crop failure in some foreign land. All of which is true, and meeting regularly with policy-makers presents an ideal opportunity for us to learn about these larger issues so that we can respond accordingly.

The motto "What's good for General Motors is good for the country" has been somewhat tarnished with the passage of time, but I've never seen a situation where honest behaviour benefiting a particular company or industry proved inimical to the best interests of the region in which it operated. Any thoughtful person recognizes the many conflicting interests that governments must balance, but we have seen time and again that selfish regional attitudes, unilateral actions, and short-term gain almost inevitably give rise to long-term pain. It's time to forge a new dynamic for the relationship between business and government, or else we all stand to lose more than we perhaps realize.

⋙•⋘

IF WE LOOK BEYOND OUR OWN small Canadian backyard, we can find some useful models for business–government cooperation. First, however, it must be said that, in my experience travelling abroad representing Noranda, I was all too often sadly disappointed in the performance of Canada's so-called "trade counsellors" who serve at our various embassies.

In the mid-1970s, for example, I met with the "forest-products counsellor" in our Paris embassy. At that time, Northwood alone shipped $10-million worth of wood products to France. The counsellor was blissfully unaware of this fact. Indeed, she had absolutely no knowledge of the company, no idea who I was, and no interest in the reason I'd turned up in her offices.

Later, when Pierre Trudeau was touting his so-called Third Option — an effort to lessen dependence on U.S. markets — the first Canadian delegation to go abroad was composed of representatives of the forest industry. I was one of the group. We ran into rough sledding right off the bat in Brussels, where the Swedes had been encamped for several years solidifying their position within the European Community and quietly negotiating advantageous quotas. I was struck by Canada's lack of preparedness on the ground. None of the Canadian representatives in Brussels had a clue what was happening, with the exception of the delegates themselves, who'd come armed with an array of facts and figures, ready to answer questions from any quarter. In vain — there was nobody to ask them. We then went to Paris, where the embassy staff still languished in ignorance. No translators had been provided for the meetings, perhaps on the overly optimistic theory that all Canadians were fluently bilingual. At that point the group proceeded to Bonn and Milan, where they encountered more of the same. I bailed out, convinced nothing would ever come of these ill-conceived perambulations.

My disenchantment with the Canadian government's failure to forge links with business at home and to adequately represent our mutual interests abroad was heightened by my exposure to how things are done in Scandinavia. I'd had occasion to visit privately a number of mills in Sweden and Finland, where I had learned a great deal. Critics are forever comparing Canada's forest operations to those in the Scandinavian countries, but there are numerous and important differences. The majority of Scandinavian timber is privately owned; holdings tend to be smaller than those controlled by Canadian firms and have been held and harvested for many more years. As a result, manmade forests are the norm. These forests are carefully tended and replanted with genetically superior stock, which translates into greatly increased yields per acre. Scandinavian forest-industry associations present a united front and are well recognized by the governments concerned. Negotiations of labour agreements, tax rules, and foreign-exchange levels take place according to long-standing protocols, which facilitate cooperative stances. A number of special tax provisions have favoured capital renewal. There's a refreshing absence of adversarial posturing between business and government; everyone is on the same team.

Nor could anyone who's seen the Scandinavian forest and mining industries in action possibly cling to the old notions of a paternalistic welfare state and cradle-to-grave coddling in a socialist utopia. On the contrary, Scandinavian governments can be pragmatic to the point of ruthlessness. Traditionally grants and loans were made available only to those firms that made a commitment to long-term modernization programs. A great many shutdowns were tolerated — indeed, encouraged or stipulated — in favour of consolidation in the form of larger, more efficient plants. In Sweden, although every effort was made to retrain or relocate workers whose jobs vanished when an outmoded mill was closed, the mill itself was actually dismantled so that no one could possibly come along and prop it up again — a course of action that should be adopted more often in Canada.

The Finns are also deserving of our close attention. They're great traders; they live or die by what they manage to export. (And import; they're taking market share away from Canadian companies in part because they successfully transplanted white spruce from the western provinces at a time when it was viewed as little more than a weed species.) It's true that Noranda traded successfully in 120 countries and that no Canadian resource firm is a stranger abroad, but the Finns have an edge, as I learned while travelling with a Finnish acquaintance to Hungary, Turkey, France, and Germany. Everywhere we went the Finnish forest-trade agent — who was often the Finnish consul, as well — would be at the airport to greet us on arrival and smooth my companion's path. The Finns had decided, correctly, that national and commercial interests are inextricably entwined.

Canada's trade representatives, on the other hand, believed that they had to maintain an arm's-length position for fear they'd be seen to favour one company over another. By doing so, they ensured only that another country would be favoured over Canada.

Other examples spring to mind. In the late 1970s and early 1980s, while Canadian firms faced a triple whammy of high inflation, high interest rates, and a sky-high dollar, the Swedish government moved to devalue the krona, thus conferring an instant advantage on Swedish exporters, particularly the pulp-and-paper producers. At the same time, it struck a deal with business and labour, under which wages were frozen — on the condition that profits would remain untaxed if channelled directly into capital investment. This arrangement was fine while it lasted, but fell apart in the later 1980s, in part because the government gave way to the wage demands of its own employees. Once I asked the Swedish finance minister if he'd follow the same policy again if circumstances warranted. He said that he would but that his mistake — one he didn't intend to repeat — was in failing to put a cap on the civil service.

Ask anyone who's travelled widely which nation, all things considered, is the best governed in the world. The answer is usually Switzerland. That's because, simply put, the country works. Its many public amenities are — well managed, well maintained, reliable, and safe. The people are prosperous and well educated, and so on and so forth. Then ask who makes Switzerland work so well? Of course it's the Swiss themselves, who make informed choices, delegating power wisely at the polls, but who are the political leaders who exercise that power? That answer is somewhat harder to come by, because Swiss politicians are in the main breathtakingly anonymous. Nobody knows their names, because they don't remain in office all that long. There's a six-year term limit across the board, and the president is out after two kicks at the can. All major policy is decided by referendum or plebiscite; thus, the people get what they want, and the politicians can't buy themselves another term, because there usually isn't one. Swiss budgets are balanced, public priorities are met, and fresh political leadership is guaranteed. Indeed, the Swiss have a long-standing tradition of public service, as opposed to the idea of politics as a career, an endless sojourn at the public trough, culminating in a senate appointment, or at least a gilt-edged pension till death do they part. Plenty of desirable candidates are willing to take their turn, knowing that afterwards they can step back into real life with a sense of justifiable pride in a close-ended job well done.

Canadian workers also have something to learn from their European brethren. I once faulted Canadian sawmill employees for rejecting a $27,000 salary offer because their peers at another firm were getting $32,000, with the result that they wound up earning $11,000 on welfare. At the time, North American forest producers had a zero profit margin, while Swedish firms were realizing fourteen percent. Another liability the Canadian economy faces is that, according to some studies, up to twenty percent of the population is functionally illiterate, a state defined as the inability to read the instructions on the label of an unfamiliar product or to tell the difference between products packaged in similar ways. The idea that a fifth of a nation's citizens are so impaired is grim enough, but in certain Canadian industries the illiteracy level reaches an intolerable fifty percent. At Noranda we found that many of our workers suffered from this shortcoming, and we strove to identify and counsel them in a considerate and nonthreatening way. This, too, was a cost of doing business. While our competitors in other countries weren't necessarily staffed top to bottom by rocket scientists, I do know that Scandinavian firms in particular reaped the benefits of more demanding educational systems, which in turn produced better-disciplined workers who proved more attuned to business realities.

I think back on various periods when the forest industry was awash in red ink, but labour told us they wouldn't give up their gains. Their position was why take cutbacks to pay for a recession they didn't create? Well, the fact is that nobody sets out to create recessions, but they keep on coming, anyway. Common sense informs us what we have to do. No intelligent person in any industry would claim that wage rates per se spell ruination — but they do contribute to or accelerate an industry's decline if they're uncompetitive and unsustainably high. Not only that, wage rates in one sector act as a bellwether to other fields, producing an inexorable upward spiral that increases input costs. Even in periods of plenty and profit it behooves everyone to work harder, produce more competitively, and take from the economy only what it can give.

So, at least, is the case in Canada's forest industry. Once upon a time our wood fibre was the most desirable in the world. Trees could be harvested with relative ease and converted by means of relatively cheap power sources. During the 1960s and 1970s, our competitors looked to Canada as the leading practitioner of log-handling, kraft-pulp technology, and newsprint manufacture. Nor did the industry rest on its laurels. Canada's plants were among the most modern and efficient to be found. Often they incorporated new technologies developed here at home; important advances sprang from Canadian research.

For a time Canadian producers managed to overcome the everlasting stumbling-blocks of climate and distance — no mean achievement when you think about what it's like to log in twenty-below weather and haul what you've cut two hundred kilometres to an unheated plant. Now compare this with the congenial prospect of logging on a tree farm in the American sunbelt or in South America, where the trees grow faster and workers are paid a fraction of the average Canadian salary. Not only that, our logging practices are constrained by factors undreamt of thirty years ago — the thorny issues of ecosystems and biodiversity, tourism, native land claims, and wilderness preservation. I don't object to any of these things, but they don't come free, and they aren't at the top of some of our competitors' agendas.

Improved technology means that once-undesirable tree species grown in other countries can be converted into first-class paper that rivals the best Canada has to offer. This isn't a temporary blip in the graph, a passing threat that will recede in time. The heyday of Canadian forest producers will not return, and the papers of tomorrow, to cite one example, will be derived from many different species, making use of a large percentage of recycled fibre and various fillers and coatings. We have lost our traditional quality advantage because the products on which we built our markets can be more or less replicated at lower cost elsewhere. This is the new competitive reality, like it or not. Our only hope is to play to our strengths: to identify and aggressively seek and confirm new markets, while maintaining our traditional base by means of an emphasis on service and attention to detail. The same basic prescription holds true for any industry providing any product of any kind. If we don't follow it, be assured that someone else will.

12

| *Envoi*

On November 1, 1995, the front page of the *Toronto Star* carried a most remarkable story. It concerned a worthy program called Take Our Kids to Work, which encourages parents to do so for one day of the school year. The program operates province-wide and is organized by The Learning Partnership, a coalition of business, school, and community groups. More than eighty percent of Ontario's 150,000 grade-nine students had registered to take part in last year's activities, perhaps on the theory that anything was better than sitting around a classroom. Those kids who couldn't for some reason accompany a parent, or whose parent had no work to go to, or who wanted to know about another line of work, were matched up with volunteers from local companies and service agencies. Teachers had been asked to prepare the kids by talking about their career hopes and the demands of a changing workplace. After the day in the workplace, there'd be a sort of debriefing to find out how the kids' preconceptions had been changed, and what they'd gathered from the whole experience.

Enter the president of one local of the Ontario Secondary School Teachers' Federation (OSSTF). This local's executive committee had passed a motion opposing the program, and their reasons were explored under the headline "Teachers' Union Wants Business Out of Education."

According to the local president, the story read, "Corporations have an agenda, and we don't want it foisted on education." He added that business "wants to gain a foothold in the classroom in order to influence curriculum and sell products." In a triumph of bad editing, the story then made a murky reference to "appeals" put forward either by the businesses involved or by teachers who disagreed with their union's position and wanted students to participate in the program. Whatever these appeals in fact were, the president, having conceded that they were "legal," termed them a "moral and ethical issue." The story quoted him saying that renegade teachers wouldn't be disciplined if they abandoned their students to the clutches of corporate greed. He added that the school district had set up an "alternative program" of its own, in which children were taken to the Metro Labour Education Centre, then to the Daily Bread Food Bank.

I have several reactions to this story.

First, I am offended by the proposition that some malign influence could possibly flow from a workplace to a child accompanying a parent there.

Second, I am saddened that such a highly dubious proposition would appear to be what many children in this school district are learning, day by day.

Third, I am depressed by the notion that it is any more virtuous to work at a food bank than in a bank. I am pretty sure that food banks everywhere are staffed and supplied by volunteers and contributors who work in financial institutions and businesses of every kind. These people give freely of their time and money; they donate goods that help sustain the less fortunate. They do so in the hopes that there will be a time when food banks will be unnecessary.

Fourth, I am appalled by the bias of the local president's argument. He talks darkly about business gaining a foothold in the classroom, but he himself is in the "business" of educating young people. He does not work free. His pension plan is the envy of the majority of Canadians. He is a public servant and he abuses his trust with these extraordinary comments — which are of course themselves an attempt to foist a particular agenda on education.

Fifth, I acknowledge the fact that, on one point, he is quite correct. The vile truth has been exposed — corporations do have an agenda. Unfortunately for the local president, however, there is nothing hidden or conspiratorial about the agenda of business. I've said before, and I repeat now, that the only reason anyone is in business is to make a profit. You do not embark on business activity primarily to improve the environment, to create jobs, to put a chicken in every pot, to look after the less fortunate, or to gratify a desire to pay taxes to various levels of government. You're there to make money. If you turn a profit, all manner of good things flow. If not, you won't eat, and neither will the people working for you, because they won't have a job for very long. Nor will you pay taxes, allegedly for the benefit of society as a whole.

Profit should be properly defined and defended everywhere, even in the classroom. As for business gaining a foothold there in order to influence the curriculum and sell products, I'm sure that every parent, employer, and school trustee hopes to see kids come out of school not only knowing how to read and write, but able to make choices wisely, able to dispute false claims, and able to think critically and creatively. If so, they will be prepared for the world and stand a far better chance of making money. They will be able to afford the products they need, which they will select by making wise choices. More important, they will be able to conceive the products of tomorrow, thus creating conditions of continued prosperity.

The OSSTF local president has drawn a line: business has no place in the classrooms of the nation. That line is artificial, of his own ideological making, and wrong. I've stated that future prosperity rests on our ability to make our way in the world — to make a profit in our business activities. Does that mean it all comes down to money in the end? Perhaps — to a degree we had better explore.

It is true that most things can be expressed in the common language of money. Money is the means by which the work of one person, one family, or one company in one place can be transferred and multiplied elsewhere. It is the vehicle by which company-building becomes nation-building. As a proud Canadian, I always took pride in the fact that Noranda's fortunes sprang from the motherlode in Rouyn, Quebec. When it came time to diversify and expand, we chose (besides other investments in that province) to develop potash in Saskatchewan, to build a forest-products industry in British Columbia, to modernize and expand facilities in New Brunswick. Yes, we went to the United States and abroad, but Canada was always our chief focus. We strove constantly to operate in a responsible and constructive way, always with the full and freely granted consent of the public at large, as well as the approval of our shareholders. This was, for the most part, possible within our borders. When we prospered, our industries prospered, and so did the nation as a whole.

It's often said that money knows no boundaries, that it flows to places of low risk and high return wherever they may be. The balance sheet is not a flag; a corporation is not a patriotic entity. Many maintain that the entire Canadian economy is an appendage of the United States, and that we have long since waved a rueful goodbye to economic sovereignty.

This is largely true, and industry does indeed transcend boundaries. A company's ability to compete has rather little to do with nationality per se, but everything to do with the arrangements within a given nation. So, should the worst-case scenario unfold and Quebec separates from Canada, conditions in Quebec might not, at least at the outset, be drastically different. Life would go on, for the resource industries at least. In 1976 when René Lévesque's Parti Québécois first came to power, the media besieged Alf Powis, then Noranda's chairman, asking if the company would flee the province. Powis, who was in a testy humour, replied that this would surely be the case; all the mines would be picked up and moved to Ontario early the following day.

But the truth is the majority of firms in a newly constituted Quebec would weather the storm and continue to do business under whatever regime its citizens deemed right and proper. Make no mistake: I abhor the thought of a separate Quebec. Nor do I wish to be an American or some other kind of non-Canadian. I want to be part of a proud and unique Canadian culture. Quebec is a large part of what makes us unique, and the kindness, tolerance, and generosity of Canadians have helped to maintain Quebec's distinct society — including its culture, language, and laws — in a most exemplary way. Why any such society would even think of choosing to break away from the country that nourished it, and to which it has contributed so much in return, is to me a matter of the greatest puzzlement.

Why do Canadians, both inside and outside Quebec, ceaselessly engage in actions that can only separate us? We wind up shouting across a widening gulf — business versus labour, rich versus poor, the regions versus central Canada, everybody versus the government, and so forever on. Are we programmed to self-destruct? I think ruefully of a conversation I once had with Dave Barrett, then the premier of British Columbia. I'd asked him why in heaven's name he'd taken a certain punitive course of action in respect to provincial tax legislation that affected Noranda. He replied that he held a profoundly pessimistic view of the human condition, and that the disparities between rich and poor were to his mind so deep he would do everything in his power to alleviate them. Basically he wanted to soak the rich, a philosophy that goes just so far, being predicated on the continuing ability and willingness of the rich to pony up. But at least he came out and said so. I liked Barrett and I respected his motive, but not his means. I also wondered how he proposed to press on with the redistribution of wealth if he put roadblocks in the way of those who would create it.

As we hover on the brink of the millennium, it is sometimes difficult not to subside into cynicism if not downright pessimism. Everyone can recite a private list of bogies and boondoggles. It's easy to conclude that society is doomed, that our cities are in decay, that an urban (and for that matter a rural) underclass is fated to endure welfare dependency and to slide into crime. It's strangely comforting to flirt with the notion of apocalypse. When it doesn't arrive on cue, you can congratulate yourself on a narrow escape and get on with the business of living.

I am undeniably on the side of free enterprise and the market system, but I know the faults and failings of laissez-faire economics and unbridled expansion. I do not accept at face value the mantra of growth and jobs. Is growth defined as higher profits, enlarged investment, more payments to governments, or all of the above? Is growth infinite or is there a limit? Can growth be local or regional, as opposed to national? Is there some stable level of economic activity, a sort of golden mean with which we should be content and count our manifest blessings? Development has its dark side, and I would far rather live downwind from a 1940s vintage pulp mill than in Tokyo, São Paulo, Mexico City, or Beijing.

If economic growth per se isn't a panacea for all of our problems, then we must propose an alternative.

I set out to write this book convinced that, if a thread ran through my organized thought over the years, it was the virtue of something that, for want of a better word, I call "process." I mean simply the way things work — how and by whom decisions are made, why things happen the way they do. I suppose this was a harking back to my university years. In my twenties I became highly influenced by the idea of a constructive dialectic based on facts. This would be achieved by the exercise of logic and reason, by quiet consideration, and careful discussion and informed debate among people of intelligence and goodwill, who could then arrive at an optimum solution.

I have filled up a great deal of paper proving that this is both true and false. It is false because the human species, while endlessly fascinating, is given to frailty and fallibility. Things fall apart, systems go off the rails, and people decline to act in purely logical ways — or indeed, even in their own best interests. In the softwood-lumber debate we've seen how, after initial unanimity, fragmentation destroyed what gains had been made. Takeovers are too often conducted purely for the sake of hegemony; hard questioning produces evasive answers; the profit motive drives participants to seize unfair advantage; vested interests have no interest in being divested. History teaches us that power has never been ceded voluntarily. Everyone has a position to maintain. Politicians, mandarins, union leaders, environmentalists, academics, professionals, and certainly businesspeople want to hang on to what they've got and get some more while they're at it. Only those with nothing have nothing to lose.

So it is that cohesion and cooperation remain elusive goals. In every group the loudest voice will assert itself. Going back through these chapters, I keep wondering, Why didn't he/she/they listen? But of course, he/she/they *did* listen — to their own self-interest, just like the rest of us.

Noranda made a lot of good decisions, but many opportunities were lost or impeded because of antipathy, obstinacy, obstructionism, and foot-dragging — not to mention faulty data or our old friend sheer stupidity. But the notion that a set of rules will mitigate against selfish behaviour — be it the refusal to pool information or to acknowledge competitive reality or to practise ideal corporate governance — is arrant nonsense. We're all individuals who behave as our experience and personality dictate. Ideally, if everyone were equally intelligent and equally educated, in possession of the same acknowledged and agreed-upon facts, even the most antagonistic parties could reach some kind of consensus. What in fact happens, no matter what system you strive to delineate and set in place, is that theory goes out the window. In practice, might makes right, even when it's wrong. The same time-worn mistakes will be made as history repeats itself and people act to suit their own purposes, reaching conclusions or causing decisions to be made that are demonstrably flawed and invalid. That was always the hardest thing for me to accept — the retreat into some illogical, capricious course of action that clearly flew in the face of reason and the facts. But in the cauldron of pressure politics, ad hoc commercial imperatives, and personal desires, there's always a shortcut — scoring goals by running behind the sidelines, or a capitulation to expediency and greed.

It is both notable and astounding that the most vociferous critics of corporate activity will simultaneously call upon business to do this, that, and the other thing — to modernize plants, retrain workers, set up pension funds, meet environmental standards, support worthy causes, and in general make sure the sky doesn't fall. Business strives to oblige, but even harder challenges lie ahead.

Given that the government's coffers are bare and bad public management has left us burdened by a huge debt, perhaps we shall see a certain percentage of corporate earnings appropriated and put directly toward socially desirable ends — jump-starting small firms, providing assisted housing, bankrolling job-retraining schemes, and so forth. We seem to be stuck in a sort of never-never land between free marketeers and those who'd seek to manage the economy within defined limits. I feel sure that new and perhaps cataclysmic changes await, if only to deal with the dreadful problem of the chronically unemployed. It's easy to say that reeducation and retraining will get hundreds of thousands of Canadians back into the workforce, but there has to be an incentive for them to do it, and there has to be a workplace for them to do it in.

Sweeping and unprecedented social and economic changes are

already upon us, and countless more await. While the experiences I've related in these pages might seem at first glance a celebration of business, they really represent a series of responses to change. We know that thousands of jobs are disappearing, that thousands of Canadians are unprepared for the new society, that unemployment is a bleak and demeaning circumstance that results in all manner of social woes. We don't have all the answers, if any, but we do know that business, in constructive cooperation with government and labour, is our best hope to solve these and other problems.

And business will be equal to the task. Business, like life, is a constant effort — fraught with peril and shortcoming — to shape the assets, resources, and forces of a given time to productive or profitable results. I'm not entirely certain that the companies with which I've been associated, not to mention the country in which I've lived, will survive beyond a decade in their present form. I hope so, because at Noranda we attempted to bring to everything we did a sort of enduring quality. I can only dimly imagine what tomorrow will bring. In the words of Victor Borge, forecasting is difficult, especially of the future.

It's trite to say that we've mortgaged the future, but it's also true. That's why we must moderate our claims and expectations, and work together to achieve realistic ends. We must stop endlessly debating the division of a shrinking pie and get on with creating opportunities for the generations of Canadians who will follow us, their hopes and dreams every bit as intense and shining as our own were not so many years ago.

Index